THE
DA VINCI MYTH
VERSUS THE
GOSPEL TRUTH

*Answers from history and Scripture to Da Vinci
Code claims about Jesus and Christianity*

D. JAMES KENNEDY
AND JERRY NEWCOMBE

Coral Ridge Ministries
Post Office Box 40
Fort Lauderdale, Florida 33302
1-800-988-7884
letters@coralridge.org
www.coralridge.org

Every time I see people reading The Da Vinci Code, *I have to restrain myself from running up to that person and saying, "If you think that's interesting, wait till you read the rest of story–the real story of Jesus." That's why I'm delighted to recommend this new book,* The Da Vinci Myth vs. The Gospel Truth *by Dr. D. James Kennedy and Jerry Newcombe. They counter all the lies propagated in the runaway best-seller.*

–Janet Parshall, Host of Janet Parshall's America

I have learned that when Dr. Kennedy speaks, it is wise to listen. As one who has written on The Da Vinci Code, *I welcome his superb and badly needed insights – for such a time as this. My advice: read everything he writes, including this book.*

–Jim Garlow, Ph.D., Senior Pastor,
Skyline Wesleyan Church, San Diego

Who would have ever expected that people in the 21st century would be accepting Gnostic heresies from the 2nd and 3rd century? But that is the legacy of the book The Da Vinci Code. *And that is why we need to have reasonable, biblical answers to the questions raised by the book. Dr. James Kennedy and Jerry Newcombe do just that in* The Da Vinci Myth vs. The Gospel Truth.

–Kerby Anderson, National Director,
Probe Ministries International, Host of Point of View

CONTENTS

ACKNOWLEDGEMENTS

There are so many to thank...and so little time, but let us try.

First of all, we are both grateful to our wives for all their help and their patience as we labored on the book. So thank you, Anne and Kirsti (who also edited an early version of the manuscript).

Also, I must thank my ever-efficient secretary, Mary Anne Bunker, for everything, and also we thank Nancy Britt for her help with the editing. Furthermore, John Aman, communications director, has shepherded the process from manuscript to book.

We are also grateful to our literary agent, Bill Jenson, for doing so much to get the message of this book out to a much wider audience.

Finally, we are most thankful to John Rabe in the television department, who provided tremendous insights and research help for this book. He was among the first on our staff to sound the alarm about *The Da Vinci Code*.

I

The Da Vinci Myth

"For the message of the cross is foolishness to those who are perishing, but to us who are being saved it is the power of God."

—1 CORINTHIANS 1:18

Unless you have been living on Mars, you certainly have heard of the runaway best-seller, *The Da Vinci Code*. It has dominated the *New York Times* best-seller list for more than 150 weeks—often in first place. This book has sold more than 40 million copies. Now comes a movie based on the book, almost guaranteed to be a blockbuster hit. This major motion picture, directed by Ron Howard and starring Tom Hanks (the Jimmy Stewart of our day) will no doubt get its message across to millions and millions of people who never read the book. This is a significant piece of work in our country. That is why it is important to address it.

The second reason for addressing it is because it is extremely deceitful. For example, on the front cover of the book it says, *The Da Vinci Code*, "a novel," but if you open the book and begin to read, you will see that the first word, all in capital letters, and standing all by itself, is "FACT." Well, now, is it fiction or is it fact? That first page says: "FACT…. All descriptions of artwork, architecture, documents, and secret rituals in this novel are accurate."[1]

I assure you that as you read it, you won't have a clue which it is—fact or fiction—because the author, Dan Brown, carefully mixes in facts with errors. However, he weaves these in with a fictional story that does draw you into it, and in the process of doing this, he is promoting a pagan religion.

BROADSIDE ATTACK IN NOVEL FORM

It is, indeed, a broadside attack on the basic foundations of the Christian religion and Western civilization, but it is not promoted as such. It is promoted as a novel, as a murder mystery, which it certainly is, but then there are these so-called facts, which we are told right up front are all true. That is the first lie in the book. They are not all true. There are numerous things he portrays as facts which are not facts at all.

Therefore, I think it would be well if we learned a little bit better what many of our fellow citizens have or are going to be exposed to, because it already is making a lot of people question many of the things they have believed.

I talked to a couple of Christian ladies recently, and they told me the book was wonderful, and they didn't see anything wrong with it at all. You see, therein lies the problem. Given the abysmal understanding of the average American today of history; add to that their lack of understanding of theology, and their limited biblical knowledge; mix all of that up with many factual errors; and combine it in an entire fictional novel, the result is that you won't have a clue whether what you are reading is fact or fiction. Since it sets out to demolish the basic foundations of Christianity, it becomes an extremely important matter for us.

"It doesn't really attack any of the foundations of the faith," some Christians told me. Well, in this book you have sort of a hero, who is going along trying to solve this mystery. The book opens up with a murder, and then some promise of the revelation of something incredible. Then the whole next 454 pages of sometimes-tedious reading is an effort to find the solution to all of that. This draws you into the plot, into the quest for the truth, but in doing that, you are fed a great many lies.

In addition to the hero, Robert Langdon, there is Dr. Leigh Teabing, a renowned historian—highly esteemed in the professional field of history. However, when you read what he has to say, as someone commented, he would be pulled over by the history police and remanded to History 101, because much of what he says would be recognized as nonsense by any high school student that ever studied history at all.

For example, he talks about the Dead Sea Scrolls, which he claims were found in the 1950s. Now would you know whether that is true or not? I hope so. A significant discovery of the twentieth century—they were found in 1947. In the book, his characters state as fact that they included many gospels. OK. Let's see. I wonder what all those gospels were. Actually, the fact is that there weren't any gospels in the Dead Sea Scrolls. Those documents were completely Jewish. However, Brown presents these things, and they come out of the mouth of Dr. Teabing, an allegedly accomplished historian. One historian remarked, "The history he recites would give the whole profession a bad name. But he is used to undercutting the truths of the Bible."

The book is also portrayed as a quest for the Holy Grail, and so you go through the whole book trying to find out what the Holy Grail is and where it is. It tells us that when they find the Holy Grail, they are going to find manuscripts which will destroy Christianity as we know it. Now that makes it, I think, particularly significant, since it really is a broadside against the very foundations of Western civilization and Christianity. It is, indeed, very deceitful.

Again, the book places most of these startling historical revelations in the mouth of the "historian" named Leigh Teabing, who is being dragged along all through this long quest for the answer to these riddles. Many people like a murder mystery, but in this one they don't realize that as they are drawn into the plot and carried along with the mystery, they are also having their faith in Christianity, in the Bible, in Christ, and Western civilization demolished in the process.

Therefore, it is a very dangerous book, and the movie will be even more so. It is destructive to the Scriptures, it is destructive to the Church, and it is destructive to the deity of Christ. It is, indeed, a totally foreign, pagan religion, that is being very subtly introduced through this particular book.

You know what I am going to do? I am going to tell you how it comes out. I hate it when someone does that to me, because when someone tells me who won the Super Bowl, I don't want to watch it. I am hoping to have a similar effect here. As I said, it is a quest for the Holy Grail (but I will reserve the revelation of the end for a little longer).

THE CHURCH HID THE TRUTH?

What Dan Brown says, essentially, is that there is this great plot, a conspiracy by the Catholic Church and by the Church as a whole, even involving the apostles. In this conspiracy, the great truth that Jesus had to tell the world is suppressed, and the real truth about Christianity is what is contained in these manuscripts, which is totally different from anything you have ever thought about or imagined.

Do I have your attention? So does the author, and

that is what makes it so deceitful. It bases its concept upon discoveries of some other gospels—the Gnostic gospels. They have been known for a long time, and they originated in the late second, third, and fourth centuries. Gnosticism was an anti-Christian heresy, one of the early ones, and the Gnostics wrote a number of gospels that are pseudo-gospels, such as the Gospel of Thomas, the Gospel of Philip, the Gospel of Mary Magdalene, and other such pseudo-gospels.

SPURIOUS GOSPELS

Why do we say they are pseudo-gospels? First of all, they were not written by Thomas, Philip, Mary Magdalene, or any of the other people whose names they bear. How do we know that? Philip couldn't have written his gospel unless he lived to be 250 years old or more—and so with the other writers. They are all second, third, and fourth century false pseudo-gospels. They have been thoroughly researched and examined and shown to be written several centuries after the original Gospels. Dan Brown says that there were eighty different gospels, and the Church suppressed most of them and only kept four.

To begin with, let us get the facts straight on this. There were only four Gospels in the first century—only four Gospels by those who were contemporary with Jesus, by those who knew Him or knew the facts intimately and first-hand. Matthew and John wrote their Gospels as eyewitnesses. From the beginning of Church history, it has been widely held that Mark wrote his

Gospel based on the memory of Peter. Luke tells us that as an historian, he carefully went back to investigate the sources. You can tell, for example, that he interviewed Mary, the mother of Jesus, because there is more about her in his Gospel than anywhere else in the Bible.

All of the other so-called gospels—the one on whose Dan Brown's case supposedly rests—were second, third, and fourth century productions, which claimed to be written by Philip the Deacon, or Thomas the Apostle, or someone like that. This is not possible because of their late dates, so they are fraudulent, spurious, Gnostic, heretical gospels.

Dan Brown takes these spurious gospels (and there were about five of them, depending on how you count them) and claims that they were really the original teachings of the Church, and then they later came along and put the authentic gospels on top of those and wiped out the Gnostic gospels. There is just absolutely no way, factually, that this could be true, because we have quotes from those authentic Gospels that go back to the first quarter of the second century. Numerous church historians and theologians quote the four Gospels, but not the Gnostic gospels.

GNOSTIC BELIEFS

One of the key aspects of Gnosticism is the view that matter is evil, and it was created by an evil deity, the "demiurge." Gnostic scholar Roelof Van Den Broek writes, "The Gnostic view of the world is anticosmic; the material world was only devised to be the prison of the soul"[2] Van Den Broek summarizes well the essence of Gnosticism: It is "characterized by an absolutely negative view of the visible world and its creator and the assumption of a divine spark in man, his inner self, which had become enclosed within the material body as the result of a tragic event in the precosmic world, from which it only can escape to its divine origin by means of the saving gnosis"[3]

One of the Church Fathers, Epiphanius, Bishop of Cyprus, tells what happened when he came across some Gnostic believers in Egypt, "about the same time the Nag Hammadi library was being collected,"[4]

> For I happened on this sect myself, beloved, and was actually taught these things in person, out of the mouths of practicing Gnostics. Not only did women under this delusion offer me this line of talk, and divulge this sort of things to me. With impudent boldness, moreover, they tried to seduce me themselves.... But the merciful God rescued me from their wickedness, and thus—after reading them and their books, understanding their true intent and not being carried away with them, and after escaping without taking the bait—I lost no time reporting them to the bishops there, and finding out which ones were hidden in the church. Thus they were expelled from the city, about eighty persons, and the city was declared of their tare like, thorny growth.[5]

We can find other references from the Church

Fathers refuting some of the Gnostic writings. They include Justin Martyr, Tertullian, and Irenaeus. Irenaeus (130-202 A.D.), the Bishop of Lyons, wrote *Against Heresies* to refute Gnostic beliefs and other heterodox opinions. He said, "The argument of those who maintain that this world surrounding us was made by an angel or by any other kind of power, or by another god, has no basis at all, for once a person is driven away from the creator of all things and concedes that the world in which we live was made by another or through another, he has to fall into many absurd and contradictory notions…"[6]

There is a great irony here. Dan Brown and other moderns who exalt the Gnostic Christians over the orthodox ones are buying into a worldview that denigrates the creation. If matter is evil, then sex is evil. The Gnostic document, *The Gospel of Philip* (c. 250 A.D.) says of Abraham, "[he circumcised] the flesh of the foreskin, teaching us that it is proper to destroy the flesh."[7] Now, presumably Dan Brown would reject the notion that sex or matter is evil, but his basis for rejecting the Jesus of the four Gospels is because of the Gnostic gospels. Meanwhile, the orthodox Gospels declare that God in Christ visited our world: "And the Word became flesh…" (John 1:14). At the beginning of creation, God said over and over, ". . . that it was good" (Genesis 1). In a sense, Dan Brown is picking and choosing what he wants from Gnosticism. Furthermore, some of the Gnostics were sexual libertines; others were ascetics.

THE RELIABILITY OF THE BIBLICAL GOSPELS

Talking about the first Gospels in the first century, Dr. Erwin Lutzer, author of *The Da Vinci Deception*, notes that eyewitnesses were still around when the New Testament was being written. If there was something wrong with it, it could have been challenged. For example, "Paul in I Corinthians 15 even said, in effect, 'If you don't believe in the resurrection of Jesus, remember that He appeared to 500 people, many of whom are living until this day. Go check it out.'"[8] This is not something that was written several hundred years later. These people who saw the risen Christ were still alive. Therefore, what you have in the New Testament is a dogged insistence on facts, on reality, on history, on evidence—and The Da Vinci Code is based on anything other than that.

The reason for the title is the hypothesis that Leonardo Da Vinci was in on the secret and placed clues in his art—the Da Vinci Code—that pointed to the truth for those who had open eyes. I know of no evidence that da Vinci was a believer in Gnosticism per se or Dan Brown's goddess-worshiping version of Gnosticism. But even if he were, and even if he did put clues in his art—which no reputable art critic/historian that I know of believes—so what? Leonardo lived some fourteen or fifteen centuries after Jesus walked this earth.

The Gnostic gospels are so fraudulent that if the Christian faith were based on anything so late and so flimsy, it would have been laughed out of existence years ago. For example: The Gospel of Thomas, one of the favorites we find being dredged up today, has Jesus saying things like this: "I myself shall lead her in order to make her a male and then she will be worthy to enter into your company. . . . For every woman who will make herself male will enter the Kingdom of Heaven (Thomas 114)." It is a funny thing, lots of feminists like to use that gospel, but very selectively, not wanting people to know that it absolutely blasts out of the water all feminist ideas. That, of course, they could not possibly take. I guess we could call them "Cafeteria Gnostics." So, even Dan Brown's own sources don't lead to the conclusion he was seeking.

The Da Vinci Code is a blatant though subtle broadside attack on the Bible. There is the hero, an historian, and a young lady (an ingénue, a very young and wide-eyed innocent girl) who is being introduced into this heretical religion. All of these heresies are placed in the mouth of this professional, notable, highly respected historian character named Leigh Teabing (the one about whom I said would have flunked History 101). For example, he finally gets around to giving her the truth about the Bible, saying, "The Bible did not arrive by fax from Heaven."[9] We didn't know that, did we? How many of you thought the Bible came to us by fax from Heaven? But this is a great revelation to this dear young innocent girl.

"The Bible is a product of man, my dear, not of God," because she had said, "I beg your pardon?"[10]

I had some Christians talk to me about this book recently, and they said, "Oh, it doesn't deny anything Christian." Really? How about that? "The Bible is not of God; it is of man. The Bible did not fall magically from the clouds."[11] Really? Gee, I thought I saw a book fall just the other day when it rained. Must have been mistaken.

> Man created it as a historical record of tumultuous times, and it has evolved through countless translations, additions, and revisions. History has never had a definitive version of the book.[12]

Here is another of the old saws that is used—that the Bible was, first of all, written in Hebrew, then in Greek, Aramaic, Latin, Syriac, French, and finally, in English, and that is how we have the Bible. We really don't know what it actually said, because, you know if you tell someone something, and they tell someone else, and they tell someone else, and they tell someone else, by the time you get to the tenth person or so, you won't even recognize the message that you gave to the first person.

That is very true, but totally irrelevant, because we have the message in the original Greek text. I have read it almost every day for the last forty-five years—and so do millions of others who know the Greek language.[13]

I don't rely on what someone thinks that someone told them that someone told them, and it's just third- or fourth- or fifth- or tenth-hand whispered rumors. We have the facts, and the facts have been indeed substantiated, but there in *The Da Vinci Code* is this continued attack against the Bible and the pushing forth of these Gnostic texts.

Gnosticism is early heresy. Gnosticism means

"knowledge." The word *gnosis* in Greek means knowledge. However, this is a peculiar kind of knowledge. What kind of knowledge is it? It is the coming to this saving knowledge, when you finally come to understand yourself, that you are "divine." If that doesn't remind you of something very prevalent in our day, you are not informed about what is going on in the religious world. That is a perfect description of New Age religion which, of course, is anything but Christian. It is totally fallacious, but that is the so-called knowledge of yourself that is one of the ways of getting to Heaven.

Gnosticism was a heresy that was dualistic. Again, the Gnostics believed that spirit was good, but matter was evil. They held that a lesser god, an evil god, was responsible for the creation of the world. They would never affirm what the New Testament declares—that Jesus Christ came in the flesh. He may have looked human, but in reality, He wasn't. One of the Gnostic gospels has Jesus appearing to be dying on the Cross—when in reality, He is separated from it, above the scene, laughing it off, because it wasn't really happening to the real Jesus, but to a body that He discarded, like shedding a garment.

DENYING THE DEITY OF CHRIST

Of course, *The Da Vinci Code* is also an attack upon Jesus Christ as well as the Scriptures. For example, Teabing goes on to tell this young lady that Jesus Christ is just a man, and that Christianity has said that He was God, but that was only decided by a vote at the Council of Nicea in 325 A.D. Then Teabing says, "A relatively close vote at that."[14] The Church did not believe in the deity of Christ until three centuries after He lived and died, and that by a very narrow vote.

Now it is true that at the Council of Nicea they voted on a number of aspects of Christianity. One of them had to do with the nature of Jesus Christ, because there were a group of heretics—another group called Arians from an Alexandrian theologian named Arius—who denied the deity of Christ. This view was having some impact upon a few people in the Church. Therefore, it was determined that they should act upon this matter. There were 318 bishops there at that time, and when they had discussed the deity of Christ at some length, they voted. They wanted to have it determined solidly that this is what the Church believed. According to the author, it just barely passed.

Let's look at another factual error. Of those 318, only two did not sign the statement that they believed the Nicene Creed, which states that Jesus is "God from God, Light from Light, true God from true God, begotten, not made, of one Being with the Father"[15]—that He is the divine and eternal Son of God. Two! Now that is really a very close vote: only two voted against the Nicene Council. Gee! We may have to have a revote on that. Check the hanging chads. This is just another blatant falsehood used in trying to deny the deity of Christ.

What does the Scripture—*the first century* witness— say about these things?

- "In the beginning was the Word, and the

Word was with God, and the Word was God" (John 1:1). And in verse 14, "And the Word became flesh, [this Word that was God] and dwelt among us, and we beheld His glory, the glory as of the only begotten of the Father."

• When Thomas, the skeptic, saw the risen Christ, he fell on his knees and said, "My Lord and my God" (John 20:28), the strongest term in the Greek language to describe who Jesus Christ was.

• In Hebrews, the Father refers to the Son; He is talking about angels. To the angels He said this and to the angels He said that. "But to the Son, he says: Your throne, O God, is forever and ever" (Hebrews 1:8). When God the Father, speaks to the Son, he calls Him God.

Therefore, the idea that the deity of Christ is something that was invented three centuries later is utterly unhistorical, unfactual, and unsupportable. The book is filled with errors like this.

Let's take an example from secular history. In the early years of the second century, less than a hundred years after Christ, Pliny the Younger wrote to the Emperor Trajan. He explained that he had two Christian deaconesses tortured to extract information from them about this alleged dangerous sect. They confessed that they got up early Sunday mornings and met as a group and worshiped Christ as a God and sang hymns to Him.[16] Keep in mind that this is one of the many testimonials from secular history from the first and second centuries that showed that Christians believed Jesus was divine. This example predates Nicea by more than 200 years.

The Da Vinci Code is definitely a blast against the deity of Christ, but what is it teaching? I said earlier it is the "quest for the Holy Grail." Do you know what the Holy Grail really is? It is a reference to the cup that Jesus passed around at the Last Supper. It was in front of Him, and He passed it around to the disciples that night at the Last Supper before His crucifixion. That cup has always been known as the Holy Grail.

Well, not according to our author here. When finally the quest is completed, the hero at last arrives at the place where the Holy Grail is. I let my daughter read that passage. I told her, "Honey, I want you to read the last paragraph on the last page of this 454-page book, and I am telling you right now what the outcome is. Here is the Holy Grail. Here is the outcome of the quest. Here is what the book is all about. So our hero says this, 'The quest for the Holy Grail is the quest to kneel before the bones of Mary Magdalene.'"

My daughter exclaimed, "What? To kneel before the bones of Mary Magdalene—a journey to pray at the feet of the outcast one?"

According to this book, Jesus is the first and ultimate feminist. According to this book, He was in love with Mary Magdalene; He married Mary Magdalene, and He had a daughter by Mary Magdalene. Furthermore, it was Jesus, the ultimate feminist, who wanted the Church to be completely run by women, and He appointed the first woman to take over the Church when He died. That was Mary Magdalene. Then these entire very bad apostles—the architects of the patriarchal Church—wouldn't hear of it, and so she was cast out by them.

Wait a minute. See if I have this right? Where did all of these apostles come from? Who appointed them? With whom did they walk and sleep and eat for three and a half years? It was Jesus. It wasn't some other group, and these are people coming in trying to hijack His religion—the religion of the deified feminine. No. They were His apostles that He appointed, and there isn't the slightest indication that Mary Magdalene was supposed to take over the Church or that she was thrown out. It is totally without historical foundation.

The Da Vinci Code would have us believe that original Christianity believed in the sacred feminine, and that it was a goddess religion, as found in some pagan religions, until the wicked Catholic Church came along to suppress that truth. They even kill to suppress it—have killed in centuries past and kill in the present day.

Another example, just to bring all of these facts and distorted facts and supposed facts together to support his thesis, he says, "Even the first Olympics were all done to the honor and glory of Aphrodite." Whoops. Did I miss something in my history? I thought they were done to the honor and proclaimed honor of Zeus.

Facts and history don't fit the picture Brown wants to proclaim here. My friends, according to him, if you want to have the real knowledge of yourself that is going to bring you to salvation, you have to understand: Is it faith? Is it grace? Is it love? Is it communion? What is it? It is sex, and when man has sex, it must not be considered, even out of wedlock, to be fornication or adultery or something unclean. It is the most spiritual experience, because since God is a goddess, the women represent this goddess when you have this intimate relationship with a woman, you are as close as you are ever going to come to a relationship with God.

If that is not blasphemy, I don't know what is. Well, yes, I do. In the temple in Jerusalem, in the Holy of Holies, where Jehovah resided over the Ark of the Covenant, between the cherubim, you find God visibly seen in the Shekinah glory. The Shekinah was the glory of God as it manifested itself there in the Holy of Holies. But according to our author, Shekinah was a woman. She was the companion of Jehovah, and what was going on in the Holy of Holies was sex between Jehovah and Shekinah. You could go in on special occasions and watch and participate, and this is the highest form of spirituality.

There it is, stripped naked—*The Da Vinci Code*. As I said before, given the abysmal ignorance of religion, history, and the Bible in our country today, we need to pray that many people might have their eyes opened. If someone asks you what you think about it, you might be better able now to answer.

The Da Vinci Code is saying that sex is divine. We experience God in the act. Certainly, God created sex. God created all those pleasurable feelings. When a man and woman are together in matrimony, that is even a picture of Christ and His bride, the Church. What the Bible says about sex is very different than the libertine view Dan Brown is presenting. Somebody must have edited out the Song of Solomon from Dan Brown's Bible.

I trust that out of all of this, God, who is able to turn all things to our good, will use it to give opportunities for us to share the true Gospel of the true Savior, who gave His life and shed His blood that we might be forgiven and redeemed and saved by His grace through faith. God has been pleased to make the wisdom of this world foolishness because the foolishness of God is greater than the wisdom of men, and through the preaching of the Cross we can come to know God and have the true gnosis or knowledge of the living God, through Jesus Christ, our Lord.

In the rest of this book we want to explore many of the errors of *The Da Vinci Code*—beyond just the few we have looked at. In addition, we will look at the kind of theological assumptions that have pushed for *The Da Vinci Code*. Next, we will look at why we believe the Bible is, indeed, the Word of God—and not the spurious Gnostic documents, which were rejected by the early Church Fathers. Then, we will look at the solid facts surrounding the resurrection of Jesus. The fact that He rose from the dead is the cornerstone of the Christian faith. It is based on solid historical evidence, which we will examine. After all, if Jesus rose from the dead, wouldn't that put a clincher on His divinity once and for all? That is what convinced the disciples—that is what should convince us, although some won't believe, even if a man rises from the dead (Luke 16:31). Finally, we will look at the ultimate and most important question that *The Da Vinci Code* raises, and that is: Who is Jesus?

2

Errors in
The Da Vinci Code

"For the time will come when they will not endure sound doctrine, but according to their own desires, because they have itching ears, they will heap up for themselves teachers; and they will turn their ears away from the truth, and be turned aside to fables."

—2 TIMOTHY 4:3-4

The Da Vinci Code is a novel, but it claims to be based on facts. Dr. Paul Maier makes a great point: What if you had a novel allegedly set with a World War II backdrop—only in this novel, Germany won the war? That doesn't work because that is not what happened. It is OK for a novelist to create a fictional story and even a fictional setting if he wishes. What you can't do with impunity is create a fictional foreground and fictional background, the latter of which you claim is based on fact. That is precisely what Dan Brown has done. His "fact" is just as much fiction as his fiction.

We are all entitled to our own opinions, but we are not entitled to our own facts.

Upon examination, *The Da Vinci Code* is chock full of errors. Some are unimportant; others, if true, would spell the end of Christianity. If they were true, by the way, we would be the first to abandon the faith. We do not seek to perpetuate something which is untrue. We do not seek to worship the Jesus Christ who never really was. As Paul said, if Jesus were not raised from the dead—if His body did not come out of that tomb—then our faith is vain and we are most pitied of all men (1 Corinthians 15:19).

Instead, the Christian faith rests on a very secure foundation. How firm? So firm that the apostles—the ones Jesus picked to send out into all the world—sealed their testimony with their own blood. All but John (and Judas the traitor) died a martyr's death. Historian Paul Maier pointed out about the Resurrection in our award-winning television special, *Who Is This Jesus*:

> Myths do not make martyrs, and if this story had been invented, they would not have gone to death for it. If Peter had invented the account, as he's ready to be hoisted up on a cross in

Rome, he would've blown the whistle and said, "Hold it! I'll plea bargain with you. I'll tell you how we did it if I can come off with my life."[17]

Of course, it is chic these days for some scholars to reject the resurrection of Christ. Why do they do that? Because of their underlying presuppositions. They accuse us of bias, but in reality their biases are greater. They "know" the Resurrection could not have happened, because people don't rise from the dead; therefore, Jesus did not rise from the dead.

Let's take an example. For our *Who Is This Jesus*, we interviewed Amy-Jill Levine, professor of Vanderbilt Divinity School. By her own admission, she is a Jewish professor of the New Testament who does not believe that Jesus is the divine Son of God. (Even though she does not believe that He is the Messiah, she is training future ministers.) Here is what she says about the alleged appearances of the resurrected Jesus to the disciples:

> Did they see Jesus? Yeah, I think they did. I think if you went up to Peter and said, "Did you see Jesus?" Peter would have said, "Absolutely!" Mary Magdalene, "Did you see Jesus?" "Absolutely!" Could I have caught it on a camera? I don't think so.[18]

But why does Dr. Amy Jill Levine dispute the biblical testimony about Christ's physical, bodily resurrection? She said:

> If rising from the dead means He and His own fully dead body came back to life and walked out of the tomb and said, "Hello, I am back

from the dead." I don't think so. That so strains
my sense of what is possible.[19]

In other words, the disbelief stems from a pre-commitment to the idea that such a thing simply cannot happen. In this view, because physical resurrection from the dead is pre-judged as impossible, the physical resurrection of Christ could not have happened.

Dan Brown doesn't necessarily deny the resurrection of Christ. He simply ignores it, but it is the foundation of the Christian faith. If Jesus is not risen from the dead, then Christianity is false. The Christian Church rests on a solid foundation, a foundation based on eyewitness testimony that was sealed in the apostles' own blood. We have nothing to fear from people seeking the truth. The truth is on our side.

Dr. Sam Lamerson, Knox Theological Seminary professor, disputes the claims of scholars like Amy-Jill Levine. He believes the historical evidence is on the side of the bodily resurrection of Christ. He notes all those who died without recanting that they had seen the risen Jesus.

> Those people who died did so knowing that it
> was going to be painful, knowing that it was
> going to be embarrassing, knowing that it was
> going to be terror-filled, and yet they did it any
> way, as a direct result of the fact that they
> believed that Jesus Christ was God. And they
> lived in the 1st century, and we live in the
> 21st century. And it seems to me that it is the
> height of arrogance for us to say in the 21st

century, "You, all you people who died, you were just foolish; you just didn't know any better. And, now, we scholars, we know a lot better then you do."[20]

Because of the critical nature of Christ's resurrection, we will deal with it even further in the Chapter 5 of this book.

ERRORS IN *THE DA VINCI CODE*

Here are some of the many errors in *The Da Vinci Code*. Some of these have been or will be treated at greater length in other parts of the book, but this is a summary of these many errors—trivial and otherwise. This is by no means an exhaustive list. First we will list the errors, and then we will restate them and refute them, some in greater detail than others:

• The chief murderer in the novel is a monk from the Catholic group.

• Opus Dei, which looms large in the novel, was created in 1099 by the Knights Templar, whom the Catholic Church later tried to exterminate to keep buried the secret which they had possession of—the secret which could undermine the foundation of the Church— the secret revealed in *The Da Vinci Code*.

• In *The Last Supper*, Leonardo da Vinci painted Mary Magdalene as the one next to Jesus. One of Brown's proofs is that John looks so feminine.

• "The New Testament is false testimony."[21]

• The doctrine that Jesus was divine was created by

a pagan emperor in the 4th century, Constantine, for the purposes of power.

• Constantine created the Bible.

• Constantine was a pagan.

• The Church destroyed the gospels that challenged the four canonical ones.

• There were eighty Gnostic gospels.

• There are thousands of documents besides the New Testament documents.

• The Gnostic gospels uniformly teach the "sacred feminine."

• Jesus was married to Mary Magdalene, and the Gnostic gospels teach that.

• Five million witches were murdered by the Church because of the Witches' Hammer Book.

• Christianity was based on pagan religions— such as the mystery religions. Specifically, Dan Brown states: "Nothing in Christianity is original. The pre-Christian God Mithras—called the *Son of God* and the *Light of the World*—was born on December 25, died, was buried in a rock tomb, and then resurrected in three days."[22]

This list of errors is by no means unabridged.

REFUTATION OF THESE ERRORS

Error: The chief murderer[23] in the novel is a monk from the Catholic group, Opus Dei.

Rebuttal: Opus Dei (the Work of God), a real organization The Last Temptation of Christ, founded in 1928, has no monks. In fact, the idea itself is contrary to their purposes, which is to energize Catholic lay people.

Error: The Priory of Sion, which looms large in the novel, was created in 1099 by the Knights Templar, whom the Catholic Church later tried to exterminate in order to keep the secret they had buried—the secret which could undermine the foundation of the Church—the secret revealed in *The Da Vinci Code*.

Rebuttal: The Priory of Sion was created out of whole cloth in 1956 by a French anti-Semite con man, Pierre Plantard. In 1975, documents were found in the Biblioteque Nationale in Paris[24] that allegedly proved the Priory is as old as 1099, and that Leonardo da Vinci and Isaac Newton and other luminaries secretly presided over it. These documents were proved to be fakes. Paul Maier notes, "In fact, one of Plantard's henchmen admitted to assisting him in the fabrication of these materials, including the genealogical tables and lists of the Priory's grand masters—all trumpeted as truth in *The Da Vinci Code*."[25] Yet this is one of the pillars Brown rests his case on. Brown states on p. 1, before getting into the novel:

> **FACT:**
>
> The Priory of Sion—a European secret society founded in 1099—is a real organization. In 1975 Paris's Bibliotheque Nationale discovered parchments known as *Les Dossiers Secrets*, identifying numerous Members of the Priory of Sion, including Sir Isaac Newton, Botticelli, Victor Hugo, and Leonardo da Vinci.[26]

Historian Paul Maier makes a great point about the Internet. He says if you go into any reputable library and look for information in print about the Priory of Sion, you will find virtually nothing. But if you check the Internet, you will find all sorts of dazzling websites (especially in the wake of the success of *The Da Vinci Code*).

The Knights Templar, however, was a real organization that grew out of the Crusades. It was created in 1118—not 1099 and made up of crusader monks who claimed allegiance and love to Jesus Christ. (Dan Brown turns them into pagan worshipers of the goddess and of an idol Baphomet.)

It is interesting that virtually every time Dan Brown deals with an historical figure, he corrupts their memories. That includes the Knights Templer, Constantine, Mary Magdalene, Leonardo da Vinci, Isaac Newton, and above all, Jesus Christ. Except for Leonardo (and Jesus), all the others worshiped Jesus Christ, and even Leonardo accepted Christianity on his deathbed. You wouldn't know any of that from The Da Vinci Code.

The Knights Templer grew so rich and powerful that it was eventually persecuted by the King of France (Philip the Fair), with permission of the Medieval Church. Brown claims that the knights found secret troves of documents under Solomon's temple that would undermine the Church. There is not a scintilla of evidence to support the claim. The only documents he ever refers to are the Gnostic gospels, such as the Gospel of Philip, or the Dead Sea Scrolls—which he apparently does not realize are pre-Christian Jewish documents only. Some critics even tear into the novel literature-wise, because he introduces these alleged treasure troves of documents that never get revisited in the book.

Error: In the Last Supper, Leonardo da Vinci allegedly painted Mary Magdalene as the one next to Jesus.

Rebuttal: One of Dan Brown's proofs is that John looks so feminine, but John is often portrayed in such a way in art because he was young. Go to any cathedral and look at the stained glass images of John. (Just as you can identify Peter because he is holding keys and you can tell Andrew because he is holding a Cross like an X (the kind on which he was crucified), so you can tell John by his feminine looks, and often he is holding a chalice, sometimes with a dragon popping out.) John often looks feminine. This was not unique to Leonardo. But suppose it were the case that Leonardo intentionally painted Mary Magdalene next to Jesus instead of John, because Jesus and Mary were allegedly married, and Leonardo was in on the secret, then I have two observations:

• Where is the "beloved disciple" John? He is not in the picture. Where is he? Under the table? Dan Brown's contention (based on the 1982 bestseller with a heterodox message, *Holy Grail, Holy Blood*) is absurd.

• And even if it were true that Leonardo intended to encode these anti-Church messages about the real Jesus, so what? Granted he was a genius, but what did he know while painting some 1,500 years after Jesus Christ?

Error: "The New Testament is false testimony."[27]

Rebuttal: The New Testament was sealed with the apostles' blood. They put their money where their mouth is. The Greek word for "witness"—as in the idea of witnessing to the truth about Jesus is "martyro," from whence we get the word martyr. Why? Because so many witnesses to Jesus, e.g., the apostles, were killed for testifying about what they themselves saw. Brown just glibly ignores this history and instead exalts the questionable writings of the second, third and fourth century Gnostic Christians, who were sexual libertines for the most part. (Other Gnostics were strict legalists.) We will deal with the reliability of the New Testament in an entire chapter.

Error: The doctrine that Jesus was divine was created by a pagan emperor in the fourth century, Constantine, for the purposes of manipulation: "It was all about power."[28]

Rebuttal: After the Resurrection, Christians worshiped Jesus because He was divine. They called Him *Kurios*, the Greek word for "Lord." In the Septuagint— the Greek translation of the Old Testament that Jesus and the apostles had (translated roughly 150 B.C.), the word used for Yahweh is *Kurios*. For a Jew to say that a human was Kurios was absolutely forbidden. The idea that Jesus was claiming Himself divine put Him repeatedly at odds with the temple authorities:

> Jesus answered,…. "I and the Father are one." Again the Jews picked up stones to stone him, but Jesus said to them, "I have shown you many great miracles from the Father. For which of

these do you stone me?" "We are not stoning you for any of these," replied the Jews, "but for blasphemy, because you, a mere man, claim to be God" (John 10:25, 30-33, NIV).

These words come from a first century document, the Gospel of John. Most scholars think it was written near the end of the first century. Some scholars think—with good cause—that it was written before A.D. 70, when Jerusalem and its temple were destroyed. There was no mention of these cataclysmic events (an argument from silence), but more importantly, there is reference to things as if they were still there. For example, in John 5:2, it says, "Now there is in Jerusalem..." (emphasis ours). How could this be if Jerusalem had already been devastated?

Error: The vote at the Council of Nicea, supposedly determining that Jesus was divine. No one believed that prior to Nicea.

Rebuttal: That is errant nonsense. Again, in the Gospels, written in the first century, we see that Jesus was divine. This is why He was delivered up to be crucified. The Jews accused Him of blasphemy, which is why the Jews arrested Jesus and had a "trial" among themselves:

Again, the high priest asked Him, "Are you the Christ, the Son of the Blessed?"

Jesus said, "I am," "And you will see the Son of Man sitting at the right hand of the Power, and coming with the clouds of heaven."

Then the high priest tore his clothes and said, "What further need do we have of witnesses? You have heard the blasphemy! What do you think?"

And they all condemned Him to be deserving of death. (Mark 14:61-64).

Note that in the Greek, when Jesus said, "I am," it is emphatic. We could translate it, "I AM!" (which to His hearers was a veiled reference to Exodus 3:14, when God identifies Himself to Moses as the great "I AM.")

Even Arius, the heretic (and catalyst for the Nicene Council), is closer to the truth than Dan Brown. Arius believed that Jesus was a god, a created being, who then co-created the universe with the Father. But there was a time when He was not, declared Arius. To resolve the conflict between Arianism and orthodox views, Constantine called the Council.

Let's take a moment to look at the historical back-drop. In the first three centuries of its existence, the Church was struggling for its very survival, as it suffered under ten intense waves of persecution from the Roman Empire, which eminent historian Will Durant calls "the greatest state history has ever known."[29]

Here you have the fledgling Christian Church fight-ing for its survival amid the fiercest opposition imagina-ble. The fact that Christianity survived and even thrived is an incredible miracle and a testimony to its divine nature.

During that survival mode, we don't necessarily look to most of those first three century Church fathers (apart from the apostles who penned portions of the Bible) for complete doctrinal clarity. As a new baby struggling in the world, the Christian faith was being threatened by all sides. There were no church buildings in those days or Christian broadcasting or publishing. Christianity was completely underground. The only creeds were very general. They only summarized the key doctrines, like the Apostles' Creed, reported to be from the second century. The canon of the New Testament wasn't even officially complete—although there was a de facto canon in operation that consisted of about 80 percent of the New Testament.

Then, in 313, when the Church was made legal under Emperor Constantine, doctrinal conflicts that had been simmering all along began to come to the forefront. The first key conflict revolved around the deity of Jesus Christ and, therefore, the triune nature of God. Was Jesus inferior to the Father? Was He "made" as opposed to "begotten"? In one sense, we could say the conflict was over the eternality (not deity) of Jesus Christ. That is, was He a created being, even if He was in some way divine? Was there "a time when He was not"? Those very words come from Arius (d. 336), presbyter of Alexandria, who believed that to be the case. (We can see the gist of the Arian views of Jesus' inferior divinity in the modern cult of the Jehovah's Witnesses.)

Although the understanding of the Trinity and the divine nature of Jesus is virtually universally accepted today by Christians of all denominations (not counting cult groups on the fringe), this acceptance didn't come easily, even after the Nicene Council. For half a century (from 325 to 381), a strong battle raged between Athanasius, who championed the Trinity (as we know it), and the followers of Arius, who championed a Jesus who was divine, but created. (When Constantine was finally baptized, near his death in 337, he was baptized by an Arian bishop. So at that particular point, the Arians were winning.) The orthodox formalized the traditional view of the Trinity in the Nicene Creed (325), but it was hotly contested. Yet, when the vote was finally cast, 316 bishops voted against Arius' views—only two voted with him. At some dark points in the 4th century, St. Athanasius and the doctrine of the Trinity were actually banished from the Empire, while Arianism was officially adopted.

But in the end, truth triumphed over error. "Begotten" triumphed over "made." Athanasius triumphed over Arius, who was declared a heretic.

In 381, with the Council of Constantinople, the Church settled the matter once and for all. Now, centuries later, millions of Christians the world over will affirm this Sunday that Jesus was "begotten," not "made." That is to say, tens of millions of people who bear the name of Christ, whether they understand the words they recite or not, will affirm these biblical truths from the Nicene Creed:

> We believe in one Lord, Jesus Christ, the only Son of God, eternally begotten of the Father, God from God, Light from Light, true God from true God, begotten, not made, one in Being with the Father. Through him all things were made.[30]

While the Bible does not teach the Trinity per se, nor

does it use the term, which was coined by the second century theologian Tertullian, the Scriptures declare seven basic truths from which we conclude that God is triune:

> the Father is God;
> the Son is God;
> the Spirit is God;
> the Father is not the Son;
> the Father is not the Spirit;
> the Son is not the Spirit;
> there is only one God.[31]

Those seven statements—all of which have ample Scriptural backing—are the reason Christians believe in the Trinity. Dan Brown rejects this because he rejects that Jesus is the Son is God.

Dan Brown's view that the early Christians believed Jesus was only a mortal rests on historical quicksand. From the very beginning, Christians worshiped Jesus as the Son of God. Jim Garlow and Peter Jones have compiled a list of several Church Fathers—all of whom wrote before the Council of Nicea in 325—affirming this most basic Christian doctrine that Jesus was divine. Those Fathers include: Ignatius (writing in 105 A.D.), Clement (150), Justin Martyr (160), Irenaeus (180), Tertullian (200), Origen (225), Novatian (235), Cyprian (250), Methodius (290), Lactantius (304), Arnobius (305).[32] Furthermore, one of the earliest Christian creeds was "Jesus is the Lord" (Kurios) (1 Corinthians 12:3).

Error: Constantine created the Bible.

Rebuttal: Constantine had nothing to do with the

canon of the New Testament. (We will address the canon in further detail momentarily.)

Error: Constantine was a pagan.

Rebuttal: This is debatable. Only God knows the heart, but Constantine claimed to be a Christian. He gave freedom to the Christians for the first time in the three hundred years of their existence. The fact that he was baptized on his deathbed—which Dan Brown says is because he was so old and feeble, he couldn't object—reflects historical ignorance. It was a common custom at the time for many converts to postpone baptism until they were at death's door, lest they die after having significantly sinned. (We would not agree with the custom, but no one should read anything into it that is not there.)

Error: They destroyed the gospels that challenged the four canonical ones.

Rebuttal: Not true. The only destruction of "Scriptures" related to Christianity (either biblical ones or extra-biblical ones) was done by Roman emperors in persecutions, e.g., Diocletian did that a couple years before Constantine took the throne.

The great thing about the New Testament is its degree of reliability. It is without question the best-attested book of antiquity. When New Testament scholars are examining the New Testament, what exactly are they working with? They are working with manuscripts which are, of course, handwritten copies of the original Greek text. The printing press wasn't invented until 1456. Until then, monks laboriously copied each biblical manuscript by hand, just as had been done for thousands of years before by Jewish scribes. In fact, that is the way the Torah is still copied today. Dr. Paul Maier, professor of Ancient History, notes: "There was a rule in recopying the Old Testament, for example, that if you made a mistake in the two-page segment, you began all over again."[33]

Fairly recent discoveries have helped confirm the accuracy of this tradition. In 1947, in what is now Israel, near the community of Qumran, a shepherd found scrolls that we have come to call the Dead Sea Scrolls. (Dan Brown mistakenly puts the find in the 1950s, a small error—but indicative of the larger picture: His facts are fiction. A worse error is his asserting that they include Christian documents). Found among the Dead Sea Scrolls were copies of the Old Testament book of Isaiah. Previous to this find, our earliest known copy of Isaiah was dated 10th century A.D. If we compare, say, Chapter 53 from one of the Dead Sea Scrolls with the 10th century scroll, we discover—after more than 850 years of copying and recopying—virtually no differences, and certainly nothing that changes the meaning. Paul Maier says this demonstrates, "the care with which the biblical scribes would transmit this data, the care that the monks devoted."

Similar care has been shown to the transmission of the New Testament text. In the vast majority of the texts, these minor differences don't change the meaning, nor do they call in dispute any major doctrine.

Dr. D. A. Carson, professor at Trinity Evangelical

Divinity School north of Chicago, notes: "Almost all text critics will acknowledge that 96—even 97 percent—of the text of the Greek New Testament is morally certain; it's just not in dispute."[34] The 3-4 percent "in dispute" cast no doubt on the major doctrines of the faith, all of which are established by multiple verses in the New Testament. Most of the 3-4 percent "in dispute" is minor word or spelling discrepancies or word order rearrangements (which doesn't change the meaning in Greek). That 96-97 percent text certainty is an extremely high number for any book of antiquity. The only thing coming close would be the Old Testament.

Furthermore, there are more than 5,000 whole or partial copies of the Greek New Testament. Scholars translate our modern English Bibles from these Greek New Testament texts. There are also thousands of early manuscript copies in other languages, such as Latin, Syriac, Coptic, Armenian, and so on, that are all based on the original Greek manuscripts. Because of the sheer number of the ancient manuscripts, the New Testament is unequaled among the writings of antiquity.

Dr. Bruce Metzger, retired professor from Princeton Theological Seminary and top-notch Bible scholar, says, "The very fact that there are so many copies still available from ancient times means that the degree of reliability of what has been transmitted to us in the New Testament is at a high level."[35]

When we compare the Greek New Testament with other writings of antiquity, we see how well-attested the New Testament is. For example, Julius Caesar wrote

Gallic Wars; we have ten known manuscript copies. Plato's Tetralogies? There are seven known manuscript copies in existence. The New Testament, however, is in a league of its own with more than 5,000 manuscript copies in the original Greek alone.

Outside the Bible, the best attested writings of antiquity are the writings of the Greek author Homer, with 647 total manuscripts in existence. Dr. N. T. Wright, former Canon Theologian of Westminster Abbey, remarks, "The New Testament documents are very reliable. We have better manuscript evidence for the New Testament than for any other ancient book."[36]

Furthermore, when one compares the time span between the author's date of completion and the earliest known manuscript in existence, the historical support for the New Testament is overwhelming. Caesar wrote his *Gallic Wars* some time before his death in 44 B.C., yet the earliest copy in existence is dated 900 A.D.—that is a gap of one thousand years. Plato wrote his *Tetralogies* some time before 347 B.C., yet the earliest manuscript copy is dated around 900 A.D., a time gap of 1,200 years. Contrast this to the New Testament … which was completed no later than 100 A.D., but the earliest known manuscript containing most of the New Testament is dated about 350 A.D. This means that the time gap for the New Testament is only about 250 years, and there are manuscript fragments even earlier than that.

Dr. Sam Lamerson of Knox Theological Seminary observes, "It seems to me that if you throw out the reliability of the New Testament documents, one must become an historical agnostic. If you're not going to accept that as basically historically reliable, you cannot accept any writings as historically reliable, because we do not have of them the same amount of backing that we do for the New Testament."[37]

And so N. T. Wright notes that the New Testament is in a league of its own among ancient books, including the Gnostic gospels, which are Dan Brown's key source from antiquity: "The New Testament is simply on a different scale entirely in terms of the depth and range of the manuscript evidence."[38]

Error: There were eighty Gnostic gospels.

Rebuttal: By any criterion, that number is grossly exaggerated. One liberal scholar, Dr. Bart D. Ehrman of the University of North Carolina-Chapel Hill, says there may have been 17 (5 of which are the 5 gospels found in the Nag Hammadi texts). Even if we accept that figure, 17, it is far less than 80.

Perhaps the most respected recent Bible scholar, who died a few years ago, was the Catholic Raymond Brown, editor of the massive *The New Jerome Biblical Commentary*. He was respected by liberals and moderates alike (but not necessarily by all conservatives, because he was too liberal for them). Brown says of the Gnostic writings, such as the 52 Gnostic texts (including five "gospels") found at Nag Hammadi: They were rubbish then (in the second, third, and fourth centuries). They are rubbish now.[39]

Error: There are thousands of documents besides the New Testament documents. Teabing states about

Jesus: "...his life was recorded by thousands of followers across the land."[40]

Rebuttal: Try 52—at least that is the number of the Gnostic documents found at Nag Hammadi in 1945. There are other Gnostic writings beyond the Nag Hammadi texts, but no reputable scholar would agree that there were thousands (or even hundreds) of such texts, nor were they written by eyewitnesses.

Try reading some of these Gnostic texts sometimes. They are often full of gibberish. For example, here is a portion of *The Gospel of Philip* (c. 250 A.D.)—Brown's only early source on the alleged union between Jesus and Mary Magdalene:

> The lord went into the dye works of Levi. He took seventy-two different colors and threw them into the vat. He took them all out white. And he said, "Even so has the son of man come [as] a dyer."[41]

Erwin Lutzer says of *The Gospel of Philip*: "Read this gospel and you will find it to be a rambling and disjointed work...."[42]

Returning to the idea that Christ's life and words were recorded by "thousands of followers," Dr. Gary Habermas points out that 90 percent of the population at that time in Israel was illiterate, and not all of those who were literate could write. Brown offers no evidence for these thousands of documents.

Error: The Gnostic gospels uniformly teach the "sacred feminine." That is just not true.

Rebuttal: Unlike the four Gospels, Gnostic gospels

can be degrading to women. *The Gospel of Thomas* declares that a woman cannot be saved unless God first changes her into a man (the very last verse of Thomas, 114).

In the Gospels of Matthew, Mark, Luke, and John, Jesus brings positive changes to womanhood. He allowed women to follow Him and to support His ministry. Above all, He allowed Mary Magdalene and her female companions to be the first to see Him raised from the dead (Matthew 28:1-8). Mary Magdalene, in particular, is the first eyewitness of the resurrected Jesus (John 20:10-18). This is significant—because it defied the norms. Dr. Sam Lamerson of Knox Theological Seminary observes:

> For instance, the women being the first ones who show up at the tomb. Women were not, in that day and age, looked upon very highly. All that one has to do is read first century Jewish documents and you realize they couldn't give testimony in a court of law; they couldn't report about what they had seen. Therefore, if somebody is making up a story, certainly they are not going to have the women be the ones who show up first.[43]

Jesus Christ liberated women in a special way. Richard Abanes, author of *The Truth Behind the Da Vinci Code*, remarks:

> The whole idea about the Church being against women is completely false. We have Christianity and the founder of our faith, Jesus

Christ, who did more for the emancipation and the exultation of women than any other religious leader. He allowed women to sit at His feet to learn. That was something you did not see in first century Israel. We have books of the Bible that are named after women. We have Mary Magdalene and the mother of Christ exalted in Church history and looked upon as godly individuals. We have women in the Bible being the first to give the resurrection story and preach the good news of the Gospel. So this Dan Brown/*The Da Vinci Code* idea that Christianity and the Christian church is terribly anti-woman is just false and that's a sad thing that we see being misrepresented.[44]

Error: Jesus was married to Mary Magdalene, and the Gnostic gospels teach that.

Rebuttal: There is the flimsiest of evidence for that. There is one passage in the Gospel of Philip (c. 250 A.D.) that claims Jesus often kissed Mary Magdalene on her _____.[45] Where he kissed her is obscure in the manuscript, which is Coptic translated from the original Greek. Brown mistakenly identifies it as having been written in Aramaic first. The word could have been mouth, cheek, forehead, or whatever. Even liberal scholar Karen King of Harvard, observes that this is referring to a holy kiss, that is, asexual.[46] Just like it says in the Bible, greet one another with "a holy kiss" (Romans 16:16). So even Dan Brown's sources from antiquity don't make his case for him.

Note what scholar Dr. Gary Habermas, Dean of the Philosophy Department of Liberty University, says:

> I have no problem with Jesus being married, if that is what the early texts say. [Today there are a lot of] historical revisionist views. People say, "What's revision?" Let me use a sports illustration. We talk about Monday morning quarterbacking and the idea is that we will solve in the barbershop on Monday morning what all our favorite coaches, teams, and players should have done the day before. We rewrite the script, but that's not how the script happened when I go back and watch a tape of the game. There are a lot of revisionist views out there: Jesus was married—something else. If our earliest authoritative texts tell us Jesus was married, I guess I am going have to say that too. I'm not going to go against the early data. The problem is not: Were most men in Palestine in the 1st century married? That is not the issue. The issue is not: Well, couldn't He have been married? Not the issue. Is it wrong to be married? Not the issue. The issue is: What do the early sources say? *We do not have an early source that says Jesus had a girlfriend, or Jesus had a fiancée, or Jesus was married.* No sin in that whatsoever. But that is not what the data say. So when people come back and say, "Well, what if . . . ?" What I think about that is it's a "what if?" It's an ungrounded "what if?" It's just what they say

it is. It's a "what if?"

However, with this generation, too often "what ifs" become facts, and the next thing we say is, "Wasn't Jesus married to Mary Magdalene? I think I heard that somewhere." Yeah, you heard it somewhere. You heard it over coffee in the coffee shop on Monday morning. That is what Monday morning quarterbacking is. I don't respect that kind of conclusion if it's done for scholarly reasons, because there are no scholarly reasons for accepting it (emphasis mine).[47]

Error: Five million witches were murdered by the Church because of the *Witches' Hammer Book*.

Rebuttal: First of all, even one alleged witch killed was one too many. But this number is grossly exaggerated. Paul Maier says that more recently, historians put the number somewhere between 30,000-50,000—far less than five million.[48]

Error: Christianity was based on pagan religions—such as the "mystery religions." Specifically, Dan Brown states: "Nothing in Christianity is original. The pre-Christian God Mithras—called *the Son of God* and *the Light of the World*—was born on December 25, died, was buried in a rock tomb, and then resurrected in three days."[49]

Rebuttal: Dan Brown has it exactly the opposite. The mystery religions more often borrowed from Christian themes—including the ones that Brown mentions. In ancient cultures, there was always the myth of the dying and resurrecting god—essentially "winter" and "spring." However, these are never alleged to have been real history.

In contrast, on such and such a day (some scholars, including Dr. Alan Whanger, retired professor of Duke Medical Center—believe April 7, A.D. 30), Jesus Christ was crucified and laid in a tomb in Jerusalem. He came out alive with a resurrected body in three days (as Jews count it—two days as we would count it).

Going further on the mystery religions, note what authors Carl Olson and Sandra Miesel write in their book, *The Da Vinci Hoax*:

> Unfortunately for Brown and the authors of *Holy Blood, Holy Grail*, there is little or no evidence that most pagan mystery religions, such as the Egyptian cult of Isis and Osiris or the cult of Mithras, existed in the forms described in their books prior to the mid-first century. This is a significant point, for much of the existing evidence indicates that the third- and fourth-century beliefs and practices of certain pagan mystery religions are read back into the first-century beliefs of Christians—without support for such a presumptive act.... "Far too many writers use this late source material (after A.D. 200) to form reconstructions of the third-century experience and then uncritically reason back to what they think must have been the earlier nature of the cults," writes Ronald Nash.... "The critical question is...what effect

the emerging mysteries may have had on the New Testament in the first century."

Rather than Christians borrowing from pagan mystery religions, there is evidence that some of the pagan mystery religions may have taken and incorporated elements of Christian belief in the second and third centuries, especially as the strength and appeal of Christianity became steadily apparent. "It must not be uncritically assumed," states historian Bruce Metzger, "that the Mysteries always influenced Christianity, for it is not only possible but probable that in certain cases, the influence moved in the opposite direction."[50]

Once again, Dan Brown's facts are fiction.

CONCLUSION

There are so many errors among the alleged "accurate depictions"[51] of *The Da Vinci Code* that historian and first-rate scholar Paul Maier just has to shake his head. He notes, "Detailing all the errors, misinterpretations, deceptions, distortions, and outright falsehoods in *The Da Vinci Code* makes one wonder whether Brown's manuscript ever underwent editorial scrutiny or fact-checking."[52] In a recent interview with Coral Ridge Ministries-TV on *The Da Vinci Code*, Maier says that if a student submitted papers with as many errors as found in Dan Brown's novel, he would flunk him.

Amazingly, we live in the Information Age, yet we live in an age of massive disinformation. The Bible says

Satan is the "the prince of the power of the air" (Ephesians 2:2). The Bible also says that in the end times,[53] "men will not endure sound doctrine; but after their own lusts shall they heap to themselves teachers, having itching ears" (2 Timothy 4:3). Is that not happening in our own day?

Dan Brown wants us to believe that the Catholic Church—apparently the only Christian body of which he is aware—was guilty of a great conspiracy and cover-up. If you are looking for an intriguing plot, why not consider the truth? God Almighty became a human, but we didn't recognize Him. C. S. Lewis put it very well in his classic, *Mere Christianity*:

> …this universe is at war…it is a civil war, a rebellion…we are living in a part of the universe occupied by the rebel.
>
> Enemy-occupied territory—that is what this world is. Christianity is the story of how the rightful king has landed; you might say landed in disguise, and is calling us all to take part in a great campaign of sabotage. When you go to church you are really listening-in to the secret wireless [radio] from our friends: that is why the enemy is so anxious to prevent us from going. He does it by playing on our conceit and laziness and intellectual snobbery.[54]

3

Why The Da Vinci Code Is So Popular

"The solid foundation of God stands, having this seal: 'The Lord knows those who are His,' and, 'Let everyone who names the name of Christ depart from iniquity.'"

—2 TIMOTHY 2:19

How is it that *The Da Vinci Code* has taken off and sold so well? Why are millions reading it—some of whom actually believe its alleged historical "facts"? Obviously, some just want a page-turning thriller. But it is much deeper than that. Dan Brown has tapped into a reservoir of discontent against the

Church, in particular the Catholic Church. The recent scandals involving predator priests—sometimes being protected by their bishops—plays well into Brown's hands. We see the Church getting caught in a shameful attempt to cover up. Many today grew up in the Church, Catholic or otherwise, and are discontent. Spirituality is in. Religion is out.

One reason for the popularity of the book is that it is a murder-mystery-thriller. Since it gained so many readers early on, many others wanted to read it: Success breeds success. Furthermore, it is a controversial religious novel, not orthodox in its perspective. Provocative, anti-Christian books sometimes sell well merely because of the controversy.

Another reason *The Da Vinci Code* is so popular is that it essentially gives permission for sex without restraints. Sex is a powerful force, and the paganistic worldview espoused in the novel encourages one to make up his or her own rules. Brown alleges that a corrupt, patriarchal Church placed arbitrary limitations on sex as a way to control people. Even through Alfred Kinsey's and Hugh Hefner's sexual revolution, most people understood that God, the Bible, Jesus, and the Church did not sanction "free love." (In fact, if people had followed God's ways—no sex outside the bounds of holy matrimony—millions would have been spared the downside of the sexual revolution, i.e., abortion, the exploding rates of sexually transmitted diseases, divorce, and subsequent poverty.)

What *The Da Vinci Code* does is place a stamp of

divine approval on sexual promiscuity. Brown never says directly that Jesus would approve of sexual immorality, but it is easily inferred. After all, Dan Brown's characters are saying that we need to rediscover the real Jesus, the "original feminist."[55] The story says we need to free "real" Christianity from the corruption of Peter and the male apostles (who supposedly hijacked the religion from Mary Magdalene, the rightful chief apostle). Since people (because of mankind's fallen condition) naturally want to live without rules limiting their sex lives, and since the spirituality promoted by *The Da Vinci Code* grants them permission to experience the divine through sex, it is no wonder the book is setting sales records. Maybe it's true when they say, "Sex sells."

Another reason *The Da Vinci Code* is so popular is its do-it-yourself approach to religion: Make up your own rules of spirituality. Dan Brown isn't saying Jesus is bad or wrong. He is saying the Church has been preaching the wrong Jesus. As Leigh Teabing says in the novel: "...almost everything our fathers taught us about Christ is false."[56]

ANTI-CHRISTIAN BIAS WITHIN THE CHURCH

The true conflict in this world is between God and Satan. Today, however, with Christianity under siege from all directions, what is perhaps most disconcerting is the attack on Christ from within the Church. For example, Dan Brown claims he is a Christian, but he denies the deity of Jesus. We believe he has tapped into the dissatisfaction of many former Christians—and even some professing Christians. They are individuals who, for the most part, have never experienced the new life Jesus Christ has come to give. They have never known the Lord personally. Their spiritual hearts have never been opened. Tragically, there are millions in the Church who are in that category. They have a form of godliness, but they deny the power therein (2 Timothy 3:5).

From "Bible scholars" who sit in judgment on the Word of God and throw out those parts of Scripture not popular by contemporary standards, to people within the Church who use Church tithes and resources to exalt the goddess "Sophia" over Jesus Christ, wholesale elements within the visible Church today are actually a part of the present-day attack on Christ in America. In this chapter, we will take a cursory look at this unbelief within the Church and how the popularity of *The Da Vinci Code* fits into it. Even if the whole world were to follow after this or some other error, may God be true and "every man a liar" (Romans 3:4).

THE SEMINARIES

Tragically, many of the nation's seminaries are so liberal they have abandoned historic Christianity or key elements of the faith. Many professors don't believe the Bible, the deity of Christ, His atoning work on the Cross, or His bodily resurrection. They are blind guides shipwrecking the faith of many a young people wishing to serve God, but come away from seminary as virtual non-believers.

Carl Rogers, for example, reportedly went to seminary to serve Christ. He attended Union Seminary in New York, where he abandoned historic Christianity; he went on to become the father of a branch of psychology that has turned many away from true faith. He has since learned better, but too late (for he has died).

When I set off to divinity school so many years ago, I knew nothing about seminaries. I found myself in one where about half the professors were orthodox, and the other half, neo-orthodox. That's another way of saying that about half them believed the Bible and the other half didn't. I heard the Bible attacked by these unbelievers in ways that were incredibly traumatic to a young theologian-to-be. My faith was shaken during that first year because I had a number of unbelievers for professors. Providentially, those who were believers helped me keep my head above water. In order to spare others from a similar experience, I eventually founded Knox Theological Seminary, so that the Bible would be taught as the inerrant word of God that it is.

My friend R. C. Sproul, the pastor, author, speaker, and head of Ligonier Ministries in Orlando, recalls a day when he was in seminary. One of his unbelieving professors asked in class, "How can you possibly believe in the atonement of Christ in this day and age?" Sproul thought to himself, "How can you possibly deny the atonement of Christ and be teaching in this Christian school?"[57]

More than a decade ago, on the day after Easter, the perceptive syndicated columnist, Don Feder, who is an Orthodox Jew, wrote about Harvard Divinity School.

He points out how far this school has fallen from its Puritan beginnings:

> Instead of singing hymns, they're sitting in the lotus position, chanting 'omm' at America's oldest school of theology. *The Nave's* [student newsletter] calendar reminds students that March 20 is Spring Ohigon, "a special time to listen to the Buddha and meditate on the perfection of enlightenment"...There's no mention of Palm Sunday or Passover, reflecting their insignificance at an institution where all is venerated, save Western religion.[58]

Feder has a friend studying there who told him that at Harvard Divinity School, "all religions are equal, except Christianity, which is very bad, and Judaism, which loses points where it intersects with Christianity."[59] Feder refers to it as a "poison-ivy" school.[60]

Indeed, a lot of these seminaries are theologically poisoning young people with their unbelief. While there are some excellent seminaries out there today, others are theologically disastrous. Young people considering the ministry today should be exceedingly careful before they decide where to attend seminary. Make sure it is biblically sound. Alumni of Christian universities should monitor their alma maters before blindly giving them their money. There is an attack on Christ from within many formerly Christian seminaries. Not all Christians falter in their faith, but some do when they are not prepared for the onslaught of unbelief.

ANTI-BIBLICAL "BIBLE SCHOLARS"

Meanwhile, there are numerous "Bible scholars" who undermine the Scriptures. An example from a decade ago is the so-called "Jesus Seminar," where more than seventy scholars voted anonymously as to whether they thought Jesus said the various quotes attributed to Him in the gospels. They ended up concluding that He only said 18 percent of that which He is credited with. For instance, these scholars voted—again, secretly—that Jesus never said, "I am the way, the truth, and the life. No one comes to the Father except through Me" (John 14:6). Out of the Lord's Prayer, the only thing the group definitely agreed He said was "Our Father."[61] Period!

They wrote a book entitled, *The Five Gospels*, so named because they treat the largely apocryphal Gospel of Thomas on a higher level than the four Gospels. In some ways, the Jesus Seminar evaluated Matthew, Mark, Luke, and John (1st century documents) through the grid of the Gnostic Gospel of Thomas[62] (no earlier than 125 A.D.).

Furthermore, a spate of relatively recent books has come out against the historical Christ:

Rescuing the Bible from Fundamentalism by Episcopal John Shelby Spong, former Bishop of Newark, New Jersey. I'll bet you didn't realize the Bible needed to be rescued from fundamentalists, did you? Christendom has waited twenty centuries to know that the Bible needed to be liberated from those who take it for what it claims to be—the revealed Word of God. One wag pointed out that someone needs to rescue the Episcopal

Church from Spong. He has generated a few books now that essentially deny key tenets of the historic Christian faith. His latest attack is entitled *Sins of the Bible*. Unfortunately, the former bishop is not alone.

Jesus the Man presents Jesus as a divorced father of three, who later remarries a woman bishop. The book was written by a woman professor at the Department of Divinity of Sydney University. When it came out, the book was reportedly selling "like hotcakes" in Australia and in America.[63] Even if that sales report is true for that particular volume (and I must add that I have never come across a copy), there is no doubt that in the religious book market, the evangelical volumes (that promote faith, not denigrate it) sell the best, even though they are sometimes hard to find in the secular bookstores.

Jesus: A Revolutionary Biography is an iconoclastic book written by John Dominic Crossan, a scholar and professor (since retired) at a major Catholic University (DePaul in Chicago). He views the Gospel writers as engaging in what one journalist labeled "retrospective mythmaking."[64] The book denies such essential Christian doctrines as the Virgin Birth and the Resurrection; instead, he believes it is likely that the body of the Lord was eaten by dogs.

And now comes *The Da Vinci Code*, not written by a scholar, and full of historical errors, as noted in the last chapter, and misinforming millions on the details of the historic Christian faith.

These are not obscure books with a tiny audience.

These are widely publicized books sold by major publishers. (As of this writing, Doubleday has published 40 million copies of *The Da Vinci Code*.) The tragedy is that if you go to your average secular bookstore, and you make your way to the back, where the religion section normally is (it is to the "back of the bus" for Christians today), you will generally find as many books against Christianity as you will find books for it.

You will often find more con than pro. *Christianity Today* even had a cover story once on some of these new books about our Lord, appropriately entitled, *The New, Unimproved Jesus*.[65] In one sense the anti-biblical scholarship is not new. On the other hand, it does seem to be gaining momentum, except insofar as adherents are concerned.

So how are we to come to grips with this kind of scholarship? I remember what my seminary professor, Dr. William Childs Robinson, said. (He was one of the orthodox ones.) He commented that you have to remember that you choose your scholars. There are scholars that say everything. Whom you choose to listen to determines the outcome.

I repeat: You choose your scholars. There are scholars that say everything. Whom you choose to listen to determines the outcome. While there are liberal Bible scholars who deny some or many tenets of the faith, there are, at the same time, many scholars (just as bona fide) who hold to a much more conservative position. For instance, there is a much larger group of biblical scholars than those 74 or so of the Jesus Seminar, who believe Jesus said everything that is recorded of Him in the four Gospels. But that is never going to make *Time*, or *Newsweek*, or any other magazines. They seem to only print that which is contrary to the Bible.

Father Francis Martin, a New Testament scholar who teaches at the John Paul II Cultural Institute in Washington, D.C., says: "In my opinion, having worked in this field now for about 40 years, 85 percent or more of the scholars in the United States and in Europe would not accept the basic principals of the Jesus Seminar."[66]

THE JESUS SEMINAR FROM AN ORTHODOX PERSPECTIVE

Let us delve further into the Jesus Seminar. The critical point to understand about this group is that there was no new evidence in the Scripture that drove them to their conclusions; it was rather their own liberal approach that led them to even undertake the project in the first place. The Jesus Seminar is best understood as worn out, liberal theologians who have turned to a publicist instead of the truth—the Jesus of Scripture. The late Dr. James Montgomery Boice, formerly the pastor of Tenth Presbyterian Church in Philadelphia, points out the Jesus Seminar is "really an example of liberal ministers and professors coming out of the closet. All they are really doing in public is what they do in a more private way in the classroom and in their own studies."[67] Dr. Boice points out the obvious: "Imagine a group of scholars, two thousand years from the time that Jesus lived and whose words were written down by eyewitnesses, later voting in a meeting on what Jesus really said and what He didn't. That is laughable."[68]

"It just seems like the more preposterous you can be," observes R. C. Sproul, "the more radical you can be, the easier it is to get a degree or to get a hearing in certain academic circles."[69]

"Liberal" and "unbelieving" are synonymous when it comes to theology. So the Jesus Seminar is essentially unbelieving scholars sharing their unbelief. When they ask a question like, "Did Jesus make this statement or not?" and then vote on that anonymously, as the Jesus Seminar did, what they are voting on is simply their own prejudices. There is nothing in the historic record, again nothing in the biblical manuscripts, that supports what they say. While manuscripts may differ in places when it comes to spelling or words, they are in complete agreement in virtually every point of theology.

If there are any of the various things in question, they are all listed in the "critical apparatus" of the Greek New Testament. (English translations have the same thing, saying things like "This verse is not found in the earliest manuscripts.") However, the people of the Jesus Seminar weren't dealing with the manuscript evidence; they were dealing with, frankly, their own feelings and with extra-biblical writings (primarily, the Gospel of Thomas—which the early Church decidedly rejected as Gnostic heresy).

Material in the Gospels where manuscripts differ in spelling or in words deals with maybe 3-4 percent of the text; the New Testament documents are very reliable.

Instead, what the Jesus Seminar has done is to get rid of 82 percent of the text. Textually, they stand on quicksand.

An important book rebuts the Jesus Seminar from an evangelical perspective: *Jesus Under Fire: Modern Scholarship Reinvents the Historical Jesus*, edited by Michael J. Wilkins and J. P. Moreland. Among those who have written essays for this book is Dr. Gary Habermas, author and co-author of numerous books on the historicity of Jesus Christ. In the chapter entitled "Where Do We Start Studying Jesus?," Denver Seminary professor Craig Blomberg has this to say about the group:

> The Jesus Seminar and its friends do not reflect any consensus of scholars, except for those on the "radical fringe" of the field. Its methodology is seriously flawed and its conclusions unnecessarily skeptical....The conservative nature of oral tradition in ancient Judaism, particularly among disciples who revered their rabbis' words, makes it highly likely that Jesus' teaching would have been care fully preserved, even given a certain flexibility in the specific wording with which it was reported. . . .There is a huge volume of scholarship to support the picture of Christ that Matthew, Mark, Luke, and John portray.[70]

WANING DENOMINATIONS

The more a denomination moves toward embracing these anti-biblical notions, the more it loses membership. Mainline denominations and liberal seminaries are vanishing from a lack of interest and relevance, even as we speak. Note that in 1965, there were 3.4 million Episcopalians in the U.S.[71] By 1994 that number was down to 2.4 million.[72] Note that during the same time, the U.S. population grew from 194.5 million in 1965[73] to 262 million in 1994.[74] As the population grew to 300 million by 2005, the number of Episcopalians slightly stagnated to 2.3 million.[75] Not all Episcopalians are liberal, of course, but the fact that the denomination allowed John Shelby Spong to serve as a bishop for so long speaks volumes about its lack of biblical standards. And it has only grown worse since 2003, when the Episcopal Church chose an out-of-the-closet homosexual as a bishop.

In 1980, there were 9.7 million United Methodists in the U.S.[76] Twenty-five years later, even though the general population grew significantly, the number of United Methodists dipped to 8.2 million.[77] Again, not all Methodists are liberal, but it is undeniable that there are certain liberal tendencies among some of the clergy and members.

In 1958, the combined membership of the two leading Presbyterian denominations, the Presbyterian Church in the U.S. and the United Presbyterian Church in the U.S.A., was four million.[78] These two bodies merged in 1983 to form the Presbyterian Church (U.S.A.) which today claims a membership of 2.4 million.[79] Again, not all Presbyterians in the U.S.A. branch are unbelieving, but many are. And in some areas, the denomination has veered greatly from its biblical roots. I personally have never been a part of the Presbyterian Church, U.S.A. It is too liberal for me. Instead, I am a minister with the Presbyterian Church in America, a Bible-based, Christ-centered body.

Simultaneous with the waning of the liberal denominations, the evangelical groups have been growing significantly. A study conducted in 1990 found that of the "500 fastest-growing Protestant congregations" in this country, the vast majority—89 percent—were evangelical.[80] That trend continues.

OPEN SEASON ON CHRIST

Today, there are things being said about Jesus even that would never have been said before. One Bible scholar of the Jesus Seminar had the audacity to call Jesus "a party animal"[81]—a very disrespectful way to label Him. The late founder and head of the Jesus Seminar, Dr. Robert Funk, said that Christ was "no goody two shoes."[82] What's more, *The Atlanta Journal* reports that "Jesus probably was a homeless drifting sage who ate and drank freely, was not celibate and challenged the religious customs of his day, according to the head of the Jesus Seminar."[83] Not celibate? Doesn't it seem like it is open season these days on Christians—and even Christ—the sinless, only perfect human being to ever live? Now His character is being dragged in the mud by those with the respectability of a degree behind their names.

I should point out that I have earned an M.Div. (*cum*

laude) at Columbia Theological Seminary (where former
Senate Chaplain Peter Marshall went), an M.Th. (*summa
cum laude*) at Chicago Graduate School of Theology, and
a Ph.D. at New York University in world religion, and
nowhere is there evidence that Jesus was not celibate or
that He was "a party animal." It seems that nowadays
some theological circles seem to play a game of "Can
you top this?"

In early 2006, rapper Kanye West mocked Jesus on
the cover of *Rolling Stone Magazine*. This took place at
about the same time that Muslims were rioting in the
streets of the Middle East and Europe in protest of a
series of anti-Mohammed cartoons published initially in
a Danish newspaper. There were no riots outside the
offices of the *Rolling Stone*. Christians know that Jesus
will be the one who ultimately fights His own battles.
Whenever Christians have used force to promote a supposedly Christian ideal, it has only brought reproach
and shame on the Lord. This was true of the Crusades,
the Spanish Inquisition, the Salem Witchcraft trials.

In 2006, NBC mocked Jesus Christ and Christians in
a sacrilegious program airing on Friday nights. *The Book
of Daniel* featured a pill-popping Episcopal priest with a
dysfunctional family that was sexually promiscuous.
Radio host Adam McManus described the show as
"Desperate Housewives with a Clerical Collar."[84] To top
things off, "Jesus" appeared to the priest; only this Jesus
was made in the priest's image and not vice versa. He was
more of a 1960s hip Jesus with a "do what you please as
long as you don't hurt anybody" attitude. Thankfully, the

program, which garnered few viewers and fewer advertisers, was canceled soon after it began. It was created by an ex-Catholic homosexual who admitted he had an axe to grind against Christianity. But then we ask, what is NBC's excuse?

Also in 2006, a painting in a black museum of art in New York City featured Osama Bin Laden as Jesus. To equate the Prince of Peace with such a prince of darkness reflects the level of hatred and animosity against Jesus.

Review the pop culture of the last few decades—perhaps beginning with the movie *M*A*S*H* (1970), as Don Wildmon once observed. You will see a repeated pattern of anti-Christian bias in that era. First it was Christians who were mocked. Eventually it was the Lord Himself. To wit, *The Last Temptation of Christ* and now, *The Da Vinci Code*, which has the potential for more damage. Why? Because everyone knew *The Last Temptation of Christ* was anti-Christian. Not everyone will know that about *The Da Vinci Code*.

And why is it open season on Jesus? He gives us the clue: "Light has come into the world, and men loved darkness rather than light, because their deeds were evil. (John 3:19).

MAINLINE DECEPTIONS

Unbelief has had devastating consequences on many churches today. There has been an abandonment of solid biblical teaching. This has spilled out from the seminaries to the pulpits, and now to the pews.

For example, it is disheartening to witness the rise of

the so-called "Christian" gay movement. It isn't enough for them to choose their unnatural lifestyle; but they want to retain the blessings of the Church, so they fool themselves into thinking that God somehow accepts them just as they are—in their unrepentant sin. It's not that homosexuals are worse than other sinners, but when homosexuals form churches in an attempt to find justification and acceptance from God, while they continue to practice their sin, they deceive themselves. "Gay churches" remind me of the ancient pagan temples which deified adultery and made pious prostitution the act of the day. They changed the truth of God into a lie.

Dan Brown in *The Da Vinci Code* tries to make the case that the "early Jews" practiced "ritualistic sex—*In the Temple, no less*"[85] (emphasis in the original). Not so. In fact, God instructed the Jews to destroy the Canaanites because of their wickedness (Deuteronomy 9:4). Archaeologists have confirmed the degree of Canaanite wickedness, as seen in such things as temple prostitution.[86]

Strong elements of the so-called "pro-choice" movement can be found within the professing Church. So can humanistic judges, politicians, and school administrators who participate in the attack on Christ in America, under the misguided interpretation of the "separation of church and state." There are even "Christian" ministers who are members of the humanistic People for the American Way or of the American Civil Liberties Union. Of course, we are talking about liberal ministers; nonetheless, they receive their pay from the person in the pew who gives at offering time.

Then there is the "sold-out-to-the-world-spirit" crowd—the group within the professing Church that embraces every fad that comes down the pike (the latest of which is *The Da Vinci Code*), even when it may be diametrically opposed to Christ. During news broadcasts about some new attack on Christ, there is often featured some clergyman who is found to be a spokesman on the anti-Christian side. When the film *The Last Temptation of Christ* came out, the National Council of Churches spoke out in favor of it.

In recent years, some mainstream denominations have come out with committee reports on human sexuality to be considered by the church-governing body. Some of these reports read virtually like tracts written in the heyday of the Sexual Revolution—to promote sexual sin under the umbrella of misnomers like "justice love." They condone just about every sexual perversion under the sun—in the name of Christianity. You wouldn't know there had been a downside to the Sexual Revolution and that more than 50 million Americans are suffering with a sexually-transmitted disease. (While such viral infections can be controlled, they can't be cured, and they often recur.)

And then, of course, there is what the Bible teaches about human sexuality. But to many leaders of these denominations, the Scriptures would appear to be obsolete. The Bible has been thrown out and *Playboy* brought in.

SOPHIA

In November of 1993, about 2,200 people gathered in Minneapolis for a church-sponsored "RE-imagining" conference. They were mostly women, with a handful of men. Almost all of the attendees worked for a church.

This "RE-imagining" conference was dedicated to re-imagining what God is like. It dedicated itself to rethinking Jesus, the community, and the Church. When a young member of our church heard just the title of the conference, he blurted out, "It's all right there in the Bible; you don't have to 'reimagine' anything"

The conference praised "Sophia, our Maker," (Sophia is the Greek word for "wisdom") while God the Father was met with derision. The atonement of Christ was denigrated by some of the speakers. For example, Delores Williams of Union Seminary said, "Jesus came for life and...atonement has to do so much with death...I don't think we need folks hanging on crosses and blood dripping and weird stuff."

Speaker Aruna Gnanadason of the World Council of Churches said, "In a global context, where violence and the use of force have become the norm, the violence that the cross symbolizes and the patriarchal image of an almighty, invincible father god needs to be challenged and reconstructed."[87]

This conference was funded by mainline churches. New Age ideas, lesbianism, and even goddess worship were promoted, while historic Christianity was ridiculed. Virtually all the funds for this conference came from church funds. Picture the believer in the pew donating money for the work of the Kingdom, only to have it pay for something like this. The conference climaxed with an "erotic" milk and honey celebration to Sophia (as opposed to the Lord's Supper).[88] Part of the liturgy of that celebration included this prayer: "Sophia, Creator God, let your milk and honey flow...Our sweet Sophia, we are women in your image. With nectar between our thighs, we invite a lover, we birth a child; with our warm body fluids, we remind the world of its pleasure and sensations...."[89]

Considering their degree of theological error, the "Sophists" make Mormons, Jehovah's Witnesses, and Christian Scientists look like orthodox Christians by comparison. In all of Church history, I have never read about anything that was as heretical and blasphemous as that conference was. It was the worst I have ever seen (until *The Da Vinci Code* came along). When someone would mention the Trinity, they would laugh. When someone would mention God the Father, they would boo. It was blasphemous to the worst degree, and it just shows you the depths to which some of the liberal denominations have plummeted.

They even held a similar conference, on a smaller scale, about a year later. It is into this form of spirituality that Dan Brown has tapped into and brought center stage in *The Da Vinci Code*. God is out. The goddess is in.

Fortunately, the National Council of Churches, a consortium of liberal churches (including some of those involved in the RE-imagining conference) is nothing like it was 35 or 40 years ago. They were once powerful, but now they have come close to going bankrupt. They have laid off many personnel. The same is true for many of the liberal denominations. (I heard one report that more Americans attend Calvary Chapels, part of the evangelical movement, than attend Episcopal Churches, one of the mainline denominations.) The liberal mainline denominations are all dying, and the NCC, as their cooperative agency, is going down with them.

These Sophia-worshiping activities remind me of an incident that took place the week before the well-publicized 1995 World Conference on Women, sponsored by the United Nations in Beijing, which promoted a radical, anti-family agenda. Many women, delegates from around the world, attended workshops in China the week before the conference. By far, the larger group was a coalition of feminists who stood squarely against the Bible and the Vatican on the issue of human sexuality (not to mention other areas). They claimed the Bible "teaches complete sexual freedom"—including fornication. (Whose translation are they reading?) As believers in free speech (except for the kind they don't like), they shouted down the opposition that tried to counter this lie.

Next, they gathered together for "prayer" to Mother Earth. They held hands in a circle and a delegate from Brazil said the "prayer": "Thanks to Mother Earth, for you give life. Thanks for water. People from my community decided no more crucifixion. We believe in life. We celebrate life, not the crucifixion. We are power." After that, many of them, including the late Bella Abzug, the former Congresswoman from New York, held their hands in the air and chanted, "I am power, I am power, I am power."[90] Whether these women were a part of the RE-imagining group or not, they are certainly one in spirit with this movement.

There is still a Sophia Caucus within the Presbyterian Church—certainly not the branch of which I am affiliated. Worship of the goddess is one of Dan Brown's chief messages in his book. The acceptance of *The Da Vinci Code* reflects in part the devastation that feminism—even so-called Christian feminism—has wrought.

WHAT IS THE CHURCH?

We have seen in this chapter repeated examples of unbelief from within the Church attempting to strike away at orthodox Christianity. These forces are not as prominent as they might seem, but a hostile media often exaggerates the influence or credibility of these anti-Christian church leaders. Nonetheless, how are we to understand how they can be within the Church and yet an enemy of Christ?

I think it helpful to back up for a moment and define the Church. The Church is the body of believers in whom Christ dwells (1 Corinthians 12:12-27; Romans 8:10-11). They are those redeemed by the blood of Jesus Christ (Revelation 1:5). But there is a much wider definition of the Church. The professing Church consists of some two billion people who claim to be believers in Jesus Christ. Within the "visible Church" is the "invisible Church." The invisible Church is a smaller group; it consists of those who truly have been redeemed by the blood of Christ. God, and only God, knows all those who belong in the invisible Church.

This distinction between the visible and invisible Church is creatively shown by C. S. Lewis in his fiction book, *The Screwtape Letters*. Lewis, who has been described as "the most original Christian writer of [the twentieth] century," has written a series of imaginary letters from an uncle demon, Screwtape, to his nephew demon, Wormwood. In one of these, the older devil observes:

> One of the great allies [to the demons] at present is the Church itself. Do not misunderstand me. I do not mean the Church as we see her spread out through all time and space and rooted in eternity, terrible as an army with banners. That, I confess, is a spectacle, which makes our boldest tempters uneasy. But fortunately it is quite invisible to these humans.[91]

That is about how the demons would see the visible and invisible body of Christ.

We can't know (this side of Paradise) all those who truly believe; that is why we are to work out our own salvation with fear and trembling (Philippians 2:12). Paul says in 2 Timothy 2:19, "Nevertheless the solid foundation of God stands, having this seal: 'The Lord knows those who are His,' and, 'Let everyone who names the name of Christ depart from iniquity.'"

So we don't know who is truly saved, but God does. We also know that we can have assurance of our own salvation. 1 John 5:13 says, "These things I have written to you . . . that you may know that you have eternal life." If we are truly Christians, we would then strive in our hearts to obey God's Word and bear fruit for His glory, abounding in good works. That doesn't mean we don't ever fall. It does mean we repent and get up again, if we do fall.

So, although the professing Church consists of roughly two billion people, only God knows exactly who are really His. Thus, we have within the nominal Church many non-believers who are spreading their non-belief. This is reminiscent of Christ's parable of the wheat and the tares:

> The kingdom of heaven is like a man who sowed good seed in his field: but while men slept, his enemy came and sowed tares among the wheat and went his way. But when the grain had sprouted and produced a crop, then the tares also appeared. So the servants of the owner came and said to him, "Sir, did you not sow good seed in your field? How then does it have tares?" He said to them, "An enemy has done this." The servants said to him, "Do you want us then to go and gather them up?" But he said, "No, lest while you gather up the tares you also uproot the wheat with them. Let both grow together until the harvest, and at the time of harvest I will say to the reapers, "First gather

together the tares and bind them in bundles to burn them, but gather the wheat into my barn …He who sows the good seed is the Son of Man. The field is the world, the good seeds are the sons of the kingdom, but the tares are the sons of the wicked one. The enemy who sowed them is the devil, the harvest is the end of the age (Matthew 13:24-30, 37-39).

And as the world contains the wheat and the tares, so too the visible Church contains those who are truly Christians and those who are not.

CONCLUSION

Dan Brown has simply joined a dishonorable cast of anti-Christian bigots. He is the new Celsus, the new Julian the Apostate, the new Friedrich Nietzsche, the new Martin Scorsese. His financial success may be deceiving. For Jesus asked, "For what will it profit a man if he gains the whole world, and loses his own soul? (Mark 8:36).

It is interesting to note that all of the anti-Christian bigots of this world will one day join all of humanity in acknowledging that Jesus Christ is Lord—not the goddess or Mother Earth or Mary Magdalene (who worshiped Jesus by the way, and not vice versa) or any false god. They will one day bow the knee and with their tongues confess that Jesus is Lord, to the glory of God the Father (Philippians 2:9-11).

One day Hitler will bow the knee before Jesus Christ. So will Marx, Lenin, Stalin, Mao, and Castro. One day Bishop Spong, Bill Maher, Martin Scorsese,

Madonna, and Dan Brown will bow their knee and profess with their mouth that He is Lord. For most of these people, it may well be too late (after their death, with no hope of salvation). Everyone the world over, including every "trendy," unbelieving "clergy person," will make this admission that He is the Lord. Keep that in mind the next time you hear some blasphemer spout off against Christianity.

4

The Gospel Truth

"But the word of the LORD endures forever."

—1 PETER 1:25A

In *The Da Vinci Code*, Dan Brown implies that the Christian Church rests on a shaky foundation, and that the Church—by which he means the Roman Catholic Church—will actually commit murder to keep certain things secret. He means things which could shake its foundation to the very core—things like Mary Magdalene was

Christ's secret bride. Again, if there were some strong evidence to come to light that Christianity was untrue, I would renounce it. The fact is, the Christian Church rests on a firm foundation—despite the criticisms of so many "Bible scholars."

C. S. Lewis, the great scholar of Oxford and Cambridge, once said:

> . . . when you turn from the New Testament to modern scholars, remember that you go among them as a sheep among wolves. Naturalistic assumptions . . . will meet you on every side— even from the pens of clergymen.[92]

Naturalistic assumptions—the idea that the supernatural is impossible—is the foundation of much unbelief in the Bible. If a "Bible scholar" begins with the assumption that miracles are impossible, then how can they believe the Scriptures? They will find later dates for the books of the Bible, with exact prophecies fulfilled, not because of the manuscript evidence, but because they assume it could not have been written before the event.

Such scholars assume that the supernatural cannot happen. Thus, they reject a priori (as a beginning assumption) that the parting of the Red Sea never happened. They assume that Jesus was not virgin born. They assume that since men don't rise from the dead (which they don't), then it was impossible for Jesus to have done so. Therefore, they throw out the very cornerstone of the Christian faith, the bodily resurrection of Christ, despite the testimony of eyewitnesses, a testimony they sealed in their own blood. The problem here is not the Scriptures; it is the anti-supernatural assumptions of the so-called Bible scholars.

JESUS AND THE BIBLE

Jesus believed the Scriptures to be the Word of God. When the devil came to tempt Him to abandon His mission and to seek personal power and glory, Jesus quoted Scripture (Matthew 4:1-10). One passage He quoted speaks directly about His total reliance upon Scripture: "Man shall not live by bread alone, but by every word that proceeds from the mouth of God" (Matthew 4:4, quoting Deuteronomy 8:3).

After He rose from the dead, Jesus confirmed that Moses was the writer of the first books of the law, and that the prophets spoke for God. "And beginning at Moses and all the Prophets, He expounded to them in all the Scriptures the things concerning Himself" (Luke 24:27; John 5:46-47). In John 10:35, Jesus declared that "the Scripture cannot be broken." In Luke 16:17, He stated, "It is easier for heaven and earth to pass away than for one tittle of the law to fail."

Jesus believed every word of the Old Testament, even the miracles. In Luke 17:29, He talked about the supernatural judgment on Sodom and Gomorrah, where Lot's wife was turned into a pillar of salt. In John 6:32, He spoke of the miracle of the manna from heaven, which fed the Israelites for forty years in the wilderness. In John 3:14, He recalled how those who had been bitten by snakes were cured instantly when they looked on Moses' brass serpent. In Matthew 12:39-40, He likened His death and resurrection to the miracle of Jonah being swallowed by a big fish for three days.

Theologian and author John R. W. Stott says Jesus' view of Scripture is the ultimate apologetic for its veracity. He writes:

> The overriding reason for accepting the divine inspiration and authority of Scripture is plain loyalty to Jesus . . . . If Jesus endorsed the Old Testament, setting upon it the stamp of his own approval, he also foresaw the writing of the Scriptures of the New Testament, parallel to the Scriptures of the Old Testament. Indeed, he not only foresaw it, he actually intended it, and he deliberately made provision for it by appointing and authorizing his apostles.[93]

Stott's argument is not circular, but linear.[94] He begins by assuming nothing. As he reads the historical first-century eyewitness accounts of Jesus in the Gospels, he sees that Jesus held the Old Testament to be the Word of God, and that He clearly predicted and made provision for the New Testament. Stott sums up:

> The argument is easy to grasp, and we think impossible to refute. It concerns the teaching of the Lord Jesus Christ. He endorsed the Old Testament Scriptures. He made provision for the writing of the New Testament Scriptures.[95]

Furthermore, we believe Jesus because He rose from the dead—thus giving veracity to all His other claims, including that of the Scriptures being the Word of God.

THE APOSTLES AND THE SCRIPTURES

The apostles also proclaimed their belief in Scripture. Paul described the Scriptures as the "oracles of God" (Romans 3:2). Hebrews 4:12 speaks of Scripture as a powerful weapon: "For the Word of God is living and powerful, and sharper than any two-edged sword, piercing even to the division of soul and spirit, and of joints and marrow, and is a discerner of the thoughts and intents of the heart."

Writing to Timothy, Paul gave the clearest and most comprehensive definition of Scripture found in the Bible: "All Scripture is given by inspiration of God, and is profitable for doctrine, for reproof, for correction, for instruction in righteousness, that the man of God may be complete, thoroughly equipped for every good work" (2 Timothy 3:16,17).

The early Church held the apostles in such high esteem that no book found its way into the canon of Scripture unless it was penned by an apostle (including Paul, who was called late in the process) or was the direct by-product of an apostle's input (such as Mark, which is widely believed to have received tremendous input from Peter). In the year 200 A.D. or thereabouts, the North African Christian Tertullian wrote, "We Christians are forbidden to introduce anything on our own authority, or to choose what someone else introduces on his own authority. Our authorities are the Lord's apostles, and they in their turn choose to introduce nothing on their own authority. They faithfully passed on to the nations the teaching which they had received from Christ."[96]

A CONTRAST WITH GNOSTIC WRITINGS

While the New Testament faithfully recorded the sayings and deeds of Jesus Christ, Dan Brown and others today are holding the Gnostic writings—again second, third, and fourth century writings—as superior to the first century Gospels (Matthew, Mark, Luke, and John). Note what Dr. Erwin Lutzer, author of *The Da Vinci Deception*, has to say:

> …these Gnostic gospels are so fraudulent. They are late dated, they are not written by the person who they are purported to be written by, and consequently, we have no reason to trust them. Whereas, in the Gospels of the New Testament, we do have solid historical evidence of eyewitness accounts as to what Jesus Christ said, and we know that these documents are early, because of the quotations from the Church Fathers, showing that they were already in existence in the 1st Century.[97]

In contrast, Dr. Lutzer tells us what Luke (who wrote the Gospel According to Luke and the book of Acts) went through to compose his Gospel:

> Luke tells us in the first chapter what his methodology was. He says, you know, many others have made careful investigation as to what has happened, but he says that I am investigating this, and he was in a position to be able to talk to people. There may have been other documents in existence that he used, but he carefully outlined his views of history and

how history should be done. And he was very
specific regarding the fact that what he was
writing was credible and had witnesses that
could be checked out.[98]

THE MEANING OF "INSPIRATION"

Jesus, the apostles, and God Himself, all declare that
the Bible is the inspired Word of God. But what does
"inspiration" mean? Benjamin Breckinridge Warfield of
Princeton, one of the greatest Greek scholars of all time,
put it this way:

> By it [inspiration], the Spirit of God, flowing
> confluently with the providentially and
> graciously determined work of men,
> spontaneously producing under the Divine
> directions the writings appointed them, gives
> the product a Divine quality unattainable by
> human powers alone.[99]

The esteemed Old Testament scholar and Semitic
language expert, Edward J. Young, said:

> Inspiration is a superintendence of God the
> Holy Spirit over the writers of the Scriptures, as
> a result of which these Scriptures possess Divine
> authority and trustworthiness, and possessing
> such Divine authority and trustworthiness, are
> free from error.[100]

Norman Geisler and William Nix, in their book
A General Introduction to the Bible, define biblical
inspiration in this way:

> Inspiration is that mysterious process by which

the divine causality worked through the human prophets without destroying their individual personalities and styles to produce divinely authoritative and inerrant writings.[101]

There are many people who confuse inspired with inspiring. There are those who say, "Oh, yes, the Bible is inspired," and yet so is John Milton, or Plato, or Socrates, or Aristotle, or any writer that might touch their fancy. Yet what they really mean is that many of these writers are inspiring—and with that I have no quarrel. But to say that they have been inspired by God to write His infallible will is an altogether different matter.

Perhaps the situation would be less confusing if the word inspiration (found in our comprehensive definition of 2 Timothy 3:16) had been translated differently from the Greek. "All Scripture is given by inspiration of God" is an incomplete translation. The Greek word theopneutos means "God-breathed"—that is, the Scriptures are "breathed out" by God. It is more expiration than inspiration. Probably the English translation should have said "all Scripture is breathed out by God" and the confusion with "inspiring" would at least be overcome.

THE BIBLE'S FULFILLED PROPHECIES

What evidence do we have that the Bible is inspired or God-breathed? First of all, in Deuteronomy 18:22, God tells us how we may know if a prophet is sent from Him: "When a prophet speaks in the name of the LORD, if the thing does not happen or come to pass, that is the thing which the LORD has not spoken; the prophet has spoken it presumptuously; you shall not be afraid of him."

God alone knows the future, "which turns on many slippery and very tricky ball-bearings" as one historian said. God alone can prophesy the future.

The Scriptures are unique in that in the Old Testament alone, there are over 2,000 prophecies that have already come to pass. You will look in vain for anything like this in the world. If we consider all the other religions of the world, there are twenty-six books which the followers of these religions claim to be divinely inspired—the books themselves make no such claim—and the books contain no specific prophecies.

Of the more than 2,000 prophecies found in the Bible, 333 deal with the coming of the Messiah. There is no other individual in the history of mankind whose entire life has been so prophetically and predictively detailed.

Frederich Meldau points out that as few as five simple points of identification can single out any individual from all of the 6 billion other people that live on this planet, and yet with Christ we have 333 points of identification. For example, suppose your name is Lester B. Smith, and somewhere in the world an envelope with that name and the address 4143 Madison Avenue, Chicago, Illinois, U.S.A. is mailed. It doesn't matter in what country that letter is mailed, it will ultimately come to you, because it has the five key points of identification: the country, the state, the city, the street, and your name.

Note that one point alone is not sufficient for identification. A Christian once showed an educated unbeliever one of the 333 Old Testament prophecies concerning Christ. After reading it, the skeptic said that he thought that for purposes of identifying Christ it was very weak and unsatisfactory. To which the young Christian replied, "I agree with you."

"What?" The skeptic exclaimed. "You agree with me?"

"Yes," said the Christian, "I think it is weak and unsatisfactory in the same way that I think a single thread is weak and unsatisfactory to handle any great weight and can be easily snapped. And yet if we take 333 such threads and wind them together, no man, not even the two strongest men we could find, would be able to break the cord produced by the combined threads. So it is with these prophecies. Though any of them may appear to be weak and unsatisfactory in identifying the Messiah, when all 333 of them come together, they present a case which is unbreakable."

Similarly, if I were to take one piece from a box containing a large jigsaw puzzle, which, when assembled, pictured the face of a famous individual, and I were to say to you, "Oh, I recognize this. It's Abraham Lincoln." You would not be easily convinced. But when all the pieces of the puzzle were in place, the features of our sixteenth President would be clearly delineated and it would be easy for you to recognize him.

Here are some of the prophecies Jesus fulfilled:

• He would come from the line of Abraham (Genesis 12:3, c. 1400 B.C., cf., Galatians 3:8).

• He would come from the line of Judah, of the line of Isaac and that of Jacob (Genesis 49:10, c. 1400 B.C.).

• He would be from the house of David (Jeremiah 23:5, c. 600 B.C.).

• He would be born of a virgin (Isaiah 7:14, c. 750 B.C.).

• He would be given the throne of David (Psalm 132:11, c. 1000 B.C.).

• This throne would be an everlasting throne (Psalm 45:6, c. 1000 B.C.)

• His name would be called Immanuel (Isaiah 7:14, c. 750 B.C.).

• He would have a forerunner who would proclaim His coming (Malachi 3:1, c. 425 B.C.).

• He would be born in Bethlehem and not merely any Bethlehem, because there were, in fact, two. He would be born in Bethlehem Ephratah, which was the small Bethlehem down south in Judea (Micah 5:2, c. 720 B.C.). There was a Bethlehem Zebulun in the northern extreme of Israel.

• He would live for a while in Egypt (Hosea 11:1, c. 700 B.C.).

• His birthplace, Bethlehem, would suffer a massacre of infants (as Herod slaughtered the infants when he heard of the birth of Jesus) (Jeremiah 31:15, c. 600 B.C.).

- He would be called a Nazarene (Judges 13:5, c. 1040 B.C.).
- He would be zealous for His Father's house (Psalm 69:9, c. 1000 B.C.).
- He would be filled with God's Spirit (Isaiah 61:1, c. 750 B.C.).

All of these things were written hundreds of years before He was born. Stop and think my friends. Suppose you were trying to describe the man who would be inaugurated President of the United States in the year 2764. He was going to be born in a small town, let's say in Mississippi—a town so small it wasn't even on the maps of that day, but it exists. You would have to describe this man's lineage and all of the things he would do and would have done to him during his lifetime. As in Christ's case:

- He would miraculously heal many (Isaiah 35:5-6, c. 750 B.C.).
- The blind would see (Isaiah 35:5, c. 750 B.C.).
- The deaf would hear (Isaiah 35:5, c. 750 B.C.).
- The lame would walk (Isaiah 35:6, c. 750 B.C.).
- He would draw the Gentiles to Himself (Isaiah 42:6, c. 750 B.C.).
- He would speak in parables (Psalm 78:2-4, c. 1000 B.C.).
- He would be rejected by His own family and friends (Isaiah 53:3, c. 750 B.C.).
- He would make a triumphal entry into Jerusalem (Zechariah 9:9, c. 500 B.C.).

- He would be praised by little children (Psalm 8:2, c. 1000 B.C.).
- He would be rejected as a cornerstone of the nation, which He would turn out to be (Psalm 118:22, c. 1000 B.C.).
- He would not be believed (Isaiah 53:1, c. 750 B.C.)..
- A friend would betray him (Psalm 41:9, c. 1000 B.C.) for a specific amount of money— 30 pieces of silver (Zechariah 11:12, c. 500 B.C.).

(Now this President, who shall reign in 2764, shall be betrayed by a friend for how much money? Do you know? How did the prophet know?)

- He would be a man of sorrows, acquainted with grief (Isaiah 53:3, c. 750 B.C.).
- He would be forsaken by all of His followers (Zechariah 13:7, c. 500 B.C.).
- He would be scourged and spat upon (Isaiah 50:6, c. 750 B.C.).
- His price money would be used to buy a potter's field (Zechariah 11:12, c. 500 B.C.).
- He would be given gall and vinegar to drink (Psalm 69:21, c. 1000 B.C.).
- He would suffer the piercing of His hands and feet (Psalm 22:16, c. 1000 B.C.).
- His garments would be parted among His crucifiers and would be gambled for (Psalm 22:18, c. 1000 B.C.).
- He would be surrounded and ridiculed by His enemies (Psalm 22:12-13, 16-17, c. 1000 B.C.).

- He would thirst (Psalm 22:15, c. 1000 B.C.).
- He would commend His spirit to God the Father (Psalm 31:5, c. 1000 B.C.).
- Not a bone of His would be broken (Exodus 12:46, c. 1400 B.C.).
- He would be buried with the rich (Isaiah 53:9, c. 750 B.C.).
- He would be raised from the dead (Psalm 16:10, c. 1000 B.C.).
- He would ascend to heaven (Psalm 68:18, c. 1000 B.C.).
- He would become a high priest greater than Aaron—in the order of Melchizedek (Psalm 110:4, c. 1000 B.C.).
- He would be seated at God's right hand (Psalm 110:1, c. 1000 B.C.).
- He would become a smiting scepter (Psalm 2:9, c. 1000 B.C.).
- He would rule the Gentiles (Psalm 2:8, c. 1000 B.C.).

What does Dan Brown say about all these prophecies and their fulfillment? Absolutely nothing. He just ignores them, just as he ignores Paul the apostle. Instead, Brown prefers to listen to second, third, and fourth century documents that alleged to be "gospels," supposedly written by apostles—who had been long dead.

Lee Strobel, a former skeptic, says of the prophecies Christ fulfilled that the Old Testament gives us a thumbprint: "It says that when you find the person that fits this thumbprint, that's the Messiah. That's the Son of

God, and throughout history, only Jesus Christ has had that thumbprint."[102] Strobel—who earned a law degree at Yale, used to be an award-winning legal affairs journalist for the *Chicago Tribune*—until he was confronted with the claims of Christ. He decided to apply all of his journalistic skills toward Christianity, so he could show how historically incorrect it was. But the skeptic became a believer when he studied the facts, as has happened many times down through history.

If you are a skeptic, I challenge you to study the historical facts about Jesus Christ—His death, His resurrection, and the prophecies written hundreds of years before He came that show with pinpoint accuracy that Christianity is true. Strobel has now written (with Gary Poole) his own rebuttal to Dan Brown's novel, *Exploring The Da Vinci Code*.[103]

As Strobel studied the prophecies that Jesus fulfilled, he found that they weren't easily dismissed. He writes: "The more I studied them, the more difficulty I had in trying to explain them away."[104] As he looked at the odds of any one person fulfilling these prophecies, he was stunned at the scientific evidence that Jesus was the Messiah. Strobel was shocked by the work of mathematician Peter Stoner,[105] who proved that the chance of any one person fulfilling even eight of these Old Testament prophecies was one in 10^{17} —that's 10 with seventeen zeroes after it. Strobel began to grapple with the implications of those formidable odds:

> To try to comprehend that enormous number, I did some calculations. I imagined the entire

world being covered with white tile that was one-and-a-half inches square—every bit of dry land on the planet—with the bottom of just one tile painted red.

Then I pictured a person being allowed to wander for a lifetime around all seven continents. He would be permitted to bend down only one time and pick up a single piece of tile. What are the odds it would be the one tile whose reverse side was painted red? The odds would be the same as just eight of the Old Testament prophecies coming true in any one person throughout history.[106]

If that didn't boggle Strobel's mind enough, Stoner demonstrated that the chances of any one fulfilling 48 prophecies were 10^{157}.[107] Strobel realized the incredible implications of that as well. It would be like finding "a single predetermined atom among all the atoms in a trillion trillion trillion trillion billion universes the size of our universe."[108] Lee Strobel finally did the intellectually honest thing—he recognized Jesus as the Messiah. He has now written such classics as *The Case for Christ* and *The Case for Faith*.

That Jesus of Nazareth fulfilled the messianic prophecies provides compelling evidence for the divine inspiration of the Holy Scriptures. The other 1,700 or so prophecies of the Old Testament deal mostly with the cities and nations that were in or near the land of Israel. Their future is outlined in those prophecies. The major emphasis of Scripture itself is on those thousands of specific prophecies. They are not vague, they could not have been made after the events, and they could never have been known by the people who made them.

THE BIBLE'S INDESTRUCTIBILITY

The indestructibility of Scripture is another proof that it is divinely inspired. For 2,600 years all the powers of this world have combined to destroy this book, and yet it still remains. *The Da Vinci Code* is simply the latest attack. I doubt it will be the final one.

One person has said that the indestructibility of the Bible is like the Irishman's wall. One Irishman built a wall four feet high and five feet thick around his farm. Someone asked him why he made it so thick. He replied, "If anyone knocks it over, it will be higher than it was before." Now this does not prove the Bible was written by an Irishman (as sad as that may seem for a Kennedy), but it does show the remarkable hand of God.

In 303 A.D., Emperor Diocletian, one of the last great persecutors of the Church, saw that the Bible was the source of courage for Christians who opposed his paganism. He ordered the confiscation of all Christian property and the destruction and burning of all Scriptures. Only ten years passed before Diocletian was dead and Constantine the Great had risen in his stead to sit upon the throne of Rome. He professed to trust in Christ as his Savior. He ordered the writing of many copies of the Scripture and encouraged everyone in the Roman Empire to read the Bible of the Christians.

Another former skeptic is author Ralph Muncaster.

He says of Diocletian's persecution:

> …in 303 A.D. an edict was given from Rome that anyone just possessing a Bible (they didn't have to say they believed in Jesus Christ or anything like that) —all they had to do was be holding a Bible—and they would be executed. That is how serious the Holy Scriptures were at that point in time. That shows you how important it was for the Christians to get this message out. It also demonstrates how much they believed in this historical message. So we have documents 1) that were a very important message, 2) that people were laying down their lives for; 3) that even in spite of this persecution, where they were trying to do away with these books, where people would be executed for these books, even so today we have thousands and thousands and thousands of extant copies of ancient copies of the New Testament, far more than any ancient book that we commonly regard as history today.[109]

There is an interesting irony about Diocletian. His grave somehow became the cornerstone of a Christian church. For hundreds of years, worshipers have praised Jesus Christ there. You may say that they worship Jesus over Diocletian's dead body—literally!

In the Middle Ages, sometimes even the clergy placed the Bible on a list of banned books. The Synod of Toulouse forbade anyone to possess a copy of the Scriptures.

Men, such as John Tyndale, who tried to translate the Bible into the vernacular of the people, were burned alive. John Huss, who proclaimed that the Bible was the final authority, was burned alive. John Wycliffe, who translated the Scripture into English, couldn't be burned because he died too soon; but his bones were exhumed and burned and his ashes scattered into the river. Yet that river went out into the sea, symbolic of the fact that his Scriptures would be spread to all of the nations of the world.

Queen Mary, otherwise known as Bloody Mary, ordered that anyone possessing a copy of the Bible would be burned. Five years after her edict, she was dead. Queen Elizabeth I ascended to the throne of England. During her time as queen, she ordered no less than 130 editions of the Bible published.

In more recent times, higher critics have done their best to destroy Scriptures from within. Yet never has an elephant labored longer to produce a mouse—because all of their efforts only confirmed the reliability of the Bible. Again, *The Da Vinci Code* is simply the latest attack on the Bible. In a few years, hopefully soon, it too will be viewed as a fad based on fraudulent "facts."

MANY BOOKS—ONE BOOK

The writings that comprise the Bible are a very exclusive list. That list was determined by God and discovered by man. It was a discovery that took place over time in the hearts of men and cannot be pinpointed as a single event.

Man discovered what God had determined by looking for certain "earmarks of inspiration":

1) The book had to be written by a man of God,
2) who was confirmed by an act of God,
3) told the truth about God,
4) came with the power of God,
5) and was accepted by the people.

In discovering these books, the Early Church Fathers did not use the word "earmarks," but the word "canon," which in Greek and Hebrew means "measuring rod." The books of the Old Testament were written over a period of about 1,000 years, and one of the first lists was produced by Melito of Sardis in 170 A.D.

When the Old Testament canon was in process, it was divided into three parts: law, prophets, and other writings. Naturally, it was not called the Old Testament. Even today, many call it the Hebrew Bible.

The formation of the New Testament canon was also a process of discovery—the difference being that it was written over a much shorter time. All New Testament books were written before 95 A.D., and so the New Testament canon could be recognized much sooner. Jim Garlow and Peter Jones point out: "Most scholars concur that the New Testament was essentially formed in the late second century as a reaction to the canon of Marcion."[110] Marcion was a Gnostic heretic who had been excommunicated by the Church. Garlow and Jones continue: "Marcion did not create the Canon. He gets a footnote in its history only because of his sheer audacity in trying to destroy it."[111] In effect, there was a defacto canon at work. This included the four Gospels.

Garlow and Jones say this of the four canonical Gospels:

> A Greek manuscript known as P45 and dated around A.D. 200, has all four Gospels together. The Magdelen College Greek Fragments of Matthew's Gospel is an early book that contains only the four biblical Gospels. One scholar argues that this collection comes from the first half of the second century. Another, basing his arguments on ancient writing forms, dates it as early as the first century. Whatever the case, some solid recent scholarship pushes the four Gospels much further back than what many had previously believed.[112]

The first complete canonical list of the 27 books of the New Testament appeared in 367 A.D. in the Festal letter of Athanasius of Alexandria. At that time, there was no correct order for the arrangement of the New Testament books. The order we have today was borrowed from the Latin Vulgate, the official publication of the Roman Catholic Church.

The late Dr. F. F. Bruce, a first-rate New Testament scholar and author of the book, *The New Testament Documents: Are They Reliable?*, underscored the point that the canon was more discovered to be divine than merely decreed as such:

> One thing must be emphatically stated. The New Testament books did not become authoritative for the Church because they were

formally included in a canonical list; on the contrary, the Church included them in her canon because she already regarded them as divinely inspired, recognizing their innate worth and generally apostolic authority, direct or indirectly. The first ecclesiastical councils to classify the canonical books were both held in North Africa—at Hippo Regius in 393 and at Carthage in 397—but what these councils did was not to impose something new upon the Christian communities but to codify what was already the general practice of these communities.[113]

This is reminiscent of the doctrine of the Trinity. Christian worship and belief from the beginning was in the triune God—Father, Son, and Holy Spirit. Although the word "trinity" is not in the Bible, it was part of the theology of the early Christians from the start of the Church. Not until the 4th century were the theological specifics nailed down. Again, belief in the Trinity was present from the start of the Church.

HAS THE BIBLE CHANGED?

Dan Brown says of the Bible, "…it has evolved through countless translations, additions, and revisions. History has never had a definitive version of the book."[114] I use on a regular basis *The Greek New Testament*. Again, 96-97 percent of the text is not even in question. The other 3-4 percent has minor variations, nothing impacting any major doctrines in the least. Meanwhile, the various translations of the Bible essentially show forth the different nuances that can be found in the process of translation. Dan Brown implies the Bible (or Bibles) we have are questionable. Again, his facts are fiction.

As noted earlier, the Bible, in particular the New Testament, is the most reputable book of antiquity. When writing was first done on scrolls, the copies deteriorated with time. However, a copy was made from the original scroll. When we compare the reliability of those copies and the earliest appearance, we see the New Testament stands alone among the books of antiquity.

Dr. Ravi Zacharias says, "If you compare any other literature from that time . . . the writings of Caesar, the writings of Homer . . . there is nothing that stacks up to the original dating and the nearest extant copies."[115] Indeed, the number of manuscript copies weighs heavily in favor of the New Testament, as we saw in Chapter 2. Sir Frederic Kenyon, a great scholar and author of *The Bible and Archaeology*, sums up the significance of the manuscript evidence:

> The interval then between the dates of original composition and the earliest extant evidence becomes so small as to be in fact negligible, and the last foundation for any doubt that the Scriptures have come down to us substantially as they were written has now been removed. Both the authenticity and the general integrity of the books of the New Testament may be regarded as finally established.[116]

As in the example of archaeology, this reliability

does not prove the divine nature of the Bible, but it does confirm it.

Over time, the Bible has become the most widely published book in the world. Since it has been translated and retranslated so many times, some people question if it is the same book: does it match the ancient manuscripts? This question was completely settled with a resounding "yes" when the Dead Sea Scrolls were discovered in 1947, as we saw in Chapter 2 with the example of Isaiah.

THE LIVING PROOF OF INSPIRATION

Another proof of divine inspiration is in the human heart. When the Holy Spirit takes up residence there, people know the Bible is, indeed, the living Word of God. I don't know of a single atheist who would even claim to have been improved as a human being by their atheism. But I know of millions of Christians who claim that their lives have been greatly improved by the Bible. Dennis Praeger, a Jewish radio talk host, once made a brilliant point about the transforming power of the Bible in people's lives. In a debate with a skeptic, he made this point (summarized here by Ravi Zacharias):

> If you were stranded on a street all alone at night, your car had broken down, say at 2:00 a.m. on a lonely street in Los Angeles . . . pitch black darkness, and you get out of your car and suddenly, you see ten big burley men coming out of a house and walking toward you, would it or would it not be comforting for you if you knew they were just coming out of

a Bible study?[117]

What a brilliant point, and so true to life.

Many years ago there was a young man who was converted after a profligate life. He had shown no interest in the things of the Lord, and even had a Christian friend who never opened his mouth about the Gospel, because he wrote that man off as too worldly to be converted. I was the young man who had been written off as beyond the grace of God. But as I invited Christ to come into my life, when I heard the Word of His glorious grace, He changed my life and transformed me from the inside out. A person who had no interest in the Scriptures, I was suddenly hungry for all I could get. Down through the centuries, hundreds of millions of people can attest to the same thing—people saved from a variety of backgrounds and all manner of evil.

CONCLUSION

God's Word is 100 percent inspired, reliable, and unchanging. We can count on it at all times. If we follow it, we will not be disappointed, defrauded, or destroyed.

I close with what the Bible says about itself. This is from Peter's second epistle and in the specific context, he is writing about prophecy, but what he says here applies to the whole Bible:

> Knowing this first, that no prophecy of Scripture is of any private interpretation, for prophecy never came by the will of man, but holy men of God spoke as they were moved by the Holy Spirit. (2 Peter 1:20-21)

5

How Firm a Foundation

"To whom He also presented Himself alive after His suffering by many infallible proofs, being seen by them during forty days."

—ACTS 1:3

I f Jesus Christ rose from the dead in time, space, and history, that would settle the question about His divinity once and for all. That is to say, the evidence is overwhelming—unless you reject the miraculous a priori, before you study the facts, but that is not a very objective way to approach anything.

Christianity is based on a deep foundation—a

foundation which cannot be shaken, despite all the attacks against it. The single most important event in Christianity is the Resurrection. Dan Brown doesn't argue against it per se. He simply ignores it. In this chapter we want to cover similar ground, treating the Resurrection in more depth.

COMPELLING EVIDENCE

The evidence for the bodily resurrection of Jesus is compelling. Some historians have called it the best attested event in antiquity. It is an indisputable fact that the disciples of Jesus were emboldened and transformed from scared rabbits into courageous and bold witnesses who could not be hushed up. The Resurrection is so critically important because it is the cornerstone of the Christian faith. Take away the Resurrection and Christianity crumbles like a house of cards. Some of the liberal denominations have taken it away from their statements of faith (if they have one), and their churches are withering away—for their congregations instinctively know that there is nothing there but froth, and they will not tolerate being deceived. If Christ was not bodily raised from the dead in human history, Christianity would cease to exist.

The historical bodily resurrection of Christ from the dead is unique among world religions. Confucius died and was buried. Lao-tse wandered off and died with his water buffalo. Buddha rotted with food poisoning. Mohammed died in 632, and his body was cut up and spread all over the near East. But Jesus rose from the dead. By that resurrection from the dead, He demonstrated that He was, indeed, the Son of God, with power. By His life, by His death, by His resurrection, He declares that He is God. Let's examine now the case for the resurrection of Christ.

THE RELEVANT EVIDENCE

Any case must deal with all of the relevant evidence. So, when you are dealing with the resurrection of Christ, we need to look at all the evidence.

It says in Acts that Christ "presented Himself alive after His suffering by many infallible proofs," (Acts 1:3). I want to examine seven pieces of evidence and seven theories that attempt to explain them away.

SEVEN PIECES OF EVIDENCE

First, there is the Christian Church, which is the largest institution or organization that has ever existed on the face of the earth, with membership easily passing two billion people by the end of this decade. Nothing comparable to her, or even close, has ever existed before. The Grand Canyon wasn't caused by an Indian dragging a stick, and the Christian Church wasn't created by a myth.

Historians—secular, unbelieving historians—tell us that the Christian Church began in Jerusalem in 30 A.D., the year Christ was killed, and that she began because the apostles started preaching that Jesus Christ rose from the dead. You strip everything else away from their preaching, and their main message was that Christ rose from the dead (e.g., Acts 2:23, 24).

Second, there is the empty tomb. Again, many adherents to many religions can travel to the place where the founder of their religion is currently entombed and say, "Here lies the dust of our estimable founder." You cannot say that about Christ. He is not in the grave. He is risen.

Paul Maier, professor of Ancient History at Western Michigan University, points out a significant fact about the empty tomb: "We often overlook the empty tomb. But I think the empty tomb is very important, because that is something an ancient historian can get at." In his book, *In The Fullness of Time*, Dr. Maier sites Jewish sources dating back to the first century confirming that the tomb was empty.[118] "The evidence is overpowering that the tomb was empty."

For 1,700 years there was virtually no controversy that the tomb was empty. The Jews didn't deny it. The Romans didn't deny it. Nobody denied it . . . until just recently. With our vast "rear view mirror" wisdom, we look back through more than 1,900 years and we decide, "Oh, the tomb wasn't empty." Too bad those who were there couldn't have been so smart.

Third, there is the Roman Seal. The huge rock had a rope stretched across it; the clay was fastened to the rope and to the wall of the tomb, and the Roman seal was impressed upon it. If you broke that, you broke the seal. If you broke the seal, you "incurred the wrath of Roman law."[119] The penalty was death.

Fourth, there was the Roman guard. According to

Professor Harold Smith, "A Watch usually consisted of four men, each of whom watched in turn, while the others rested beside him so as to be roused by the least alarm; but in this case the guard may have been more numerous."[120] These Roman soldiers were well-trained. They were experts in what they did. The penalty for leaving their post or for falling asleep at the job was death[121]—death that was "always rigorously enforced."[122]

Fifth, there was the stone—at least two tons, probably more. The opening would indicate that the stone would have to be at least about seven or eight feet high. It took more than one person to move it.

Sixth, there were the appearances. These are crucial. Over a period of about six weeks He appeared to one, then to another, then to two, then to three and then to eight and ten and eleven and 500 people at a time (1 Corinthians 15:4-9). They saw Him, they heard Him, they handled Him. He fixed breakfast for them. He ate fish with them (John 21:7-15; Luke 24:42-43).

The transformation of the apostles was connected to the appearances. One day they were cringing in an upper room for fear of the Jews, and soon after, they were boldly upbraiding the Sanhedrin and proclaiming the resurrection of Christ. Consider also their martyrdom. They were crucified, crucified upside down, sawed in half, stoned to death, and killed in many other ways, except for John, who was exiled to the island of Patmos by Nero. Why would they give their lives for what they knew to be false?

Seven, there is the character of Christ Himself. Christ

is universally acknowledged, even often enough by skeptics, to be a paragon of virtue, and the most noble, moral, truthful, and ethical man the world has ever seen. Even Dan Brown admits that Jesus was an "historical figure of staggering influence, perhaps the most enigmatic and inspirational leader the world has ever seen."[123] The last thing Jesus would promote would be deception, including the deception that He rose from the dead—if, in fact, He didn't.

THEORIES THAT TRY TO EXPLAIN
AWAY THE RESURRECTION OF CHRIST

As apologist Josh McDowell points out, some theories to explain away the resurrection of Christ take as much faith to believe as the Resurrection itself.[124] He has debated the Resurrection with skeptics more than just about anyone alive. He writes:

> After more than 700 hours of studying this subject, and thoroughly investigating its foundation, I have come to the conclusion that the resurrection of Jesus Christ is one of the "most wicked, vicious, heartless hoaxes ever foisted upon the minds of men, or it is the most fantastic fact of history.... A student at the University of Uruguay said to me: "Professor McDowell, why can't you refute Christianity?"
> I answered: "For a very simple reason: I am not able to explain away an event in history— the resurrection of Jesus Christ."[125]

We will now examine some of the theories put forth

to explain away the resurrection of Jesus Christ.

THE FRAUD THEORY

The first theory to explain away Christ's resurrection is called the "Fraud Theory." This was and is the theory of the Jews. Essentially, what the Jews are saying is that the whole thing was a fraud. We read: "Now while they were going, behold, some of the guard came into the city and reported to the chief priests all the things that had happened" (Matthew 28:11).

Interestingly, you hear it said sometimes that Jesus never appeared to anybody but believers. But that is not true; He appeared to the guard. They were so terrified by His appearance that they fainted and became as dead men. Then they came and told the High Priest what had happened. Jesus appeared to James, his brother, who was skeptical. Jesus appeared to Saul, the persecutor. None of these was a Christian at the time.

The Bible continues: "When they had assembled with the elders and consulted together, they gave a large sum of money to the soldiers, saying, 'Tell them, "His disciples came at night and stole Him away while we slept." And if this comes to the governor's ears, we will appease him and make you secure." So they took the money and did as they were instructed; and this saying is commonly reported among the Jews until this day" (Matthew 28:12-15) ...and until this day, nearly 2,000 years later.

How does this stack up with the evidence. First of all, there is the Christian Church. Does the "Fraud

Theory" give a plausible reason for the Christian Church? The Church was founded by the apostles, who preached the Resurrection. If the Fraud Theory were right, then they knew they had stolen the body and planted it in the rose garden. But they went ahead and proclaimed that He had risen from the dead.

Something happened to the disciples that changed them in a moment, from cowardice to heroic courage. They said it was that they had seen Jesus risen from the dead. To say that they stole the body and made up a resurrection doesn't make sense. That view does not reflect the realities of human nature. For example, when two criminals are charged with the same murder, even when they have previously been friends, they will almost invariably accuse the other of pulling the trigger.

The disciples didn't change their story one bit, although they had everything to gain and nothing to lose by doing so. The apostles continued throughout all of their lives to proclaim that they had seen Him risen from the dead. Their speaking out led to torture and execution, but none of them ever sought to save his own skin by revealing the "plot."

Dr. Principal Hill, who wrote *Lectures in Divinity*, which were popular in the nineteenth century, has shown the absurdity of the Fraud theory perhaps more succinctly than anyone else. This is terrific:

> You must suppose that twelve men of mean birth, of no education, living in that humble station which placed ambitious views out of their reach and far from their thoughts, without

any aid from the state, formed the noblest scheme which ever entered into the mind of man, adopted the most daring means of executing that scheme, conducted it with such address as to conceal the imposture under the semblance of simplicity and virtue. You must suppose, also, that men guilty of blasphemy and falsehood, united in an attempt the best contrived, and which has in fact proved the most successful for making the world virtuous; that they formed this single enterprise without seeking any advantage to themselves, with an avowed contempt of loss and profit, and with the certain expectation of scorn and persecution; that although conscious of one another's villainy, none of them ever thought of providing for his own security by disclosing the fraud, but that amidst sufferings the most grievous to flesh and blood they persevered in their conspiracy to cheat the world into piety, honesty and benevolence. Truly, they who can swallow such suppositions have no title to object to miracles.[126]

How true that is. No, the Fraud Theory will not stand up to the evidence.

THE SWOON THEORY

A second theory to explain away the Resurrection is the "Swoon Theory." This is the theory of the Christian Scientists. The Swoon Theory is the idea that Jesus never really died. It is most interesting that until the 1800s, no one ever thought that Jesus hadn't died. Everyone believed He had.

I think it is significant that the people who put Him to death were "in the business." What was their trade? Their business was taking people who were alive and making them into people who were dead. That is what they did for a living. They would go home at night and say, "Well, I did three today, honey." They were experts at what they did.

But what the Swoon theory says is that Jesus didn't really die; He merely swooned and then, being placed in the fresh coolness of the tomb, He revived. That does not live up to the facts. Obviously, here is a man who had been scourged, which often killed people in and of itself. His hands and feet and His side had been pierced.

In the Philippines, some people have had themselves crucified on Good Friday. They will sometimes stay up there for three, four, or five minutes, and then, not having been scourged, not having been up all night, not having gone without food for hours, not having had their side and pericardium pierced, they are taken down and moved to a hospital, where they very nearly die.

Jesus, we are supposed to believe, having been placed in the cool freshness of a tomb, revived. Actually, if a person has gone into shock, should you put him in a cool place? No way. That would kill him. Instead, you cover him with blankets and try to keep his body temperature up. So the cool freshness of the tomb may sound nice on a hot day, but if you are in shock, that is the last thing you want. In fact, if He were not dead when they put Him into the tomb, that most certainly would have killed Him.[127]

Supposedly, Jesus stays there for three days, and then He gets up on mangled feet, hobbles to the door of the tomb and finds there this stone weighing a few tons. With mangled hands, He presses against the flat side of the rock and rolls it away. Then He overcomes the Roman guard of armed men. After that, He takes a seven-mile hike to Emmaus and chats with some fellows on the way. No one noticed He was limping. Then He treks almost a hundred miles to Galilee and climbs a mountain. There He convinces 500 people that He is the Lord of Life.

The Swoon theory has received a fatal blow by a skeptic himself by the name of David Friedrich Strauss—a 19th century German who wrote on the life of Jesus. He didn't believe in the Resurrection, but he knew that this theory was utterly ridiculous. Listen to what an unbeliever says about the Swoon theory:

> It is impossible that a being who had stolen half dead out of the sepulcher, who crept about weak and ill, wanting medical treatment, who required bandaging, strengthening and indulgence and who, still at last, yielded to his sufferings, could have given to the disciples the impression that he was a conqueror over death and the grave, The Prince of Life, an impression which lay at the bottom of all of their future ministry. Such a resuscitation could only have

weakened the impression which he made in life and in death and at the most, could only have given it an elegiac voice, a lament for the dead. But could by no possibility have changed their sorrow into enthusiasm, have elevated their reverence into worship.[128]

And with Strauss' critique, other than the devoted Christian Scientists, the Swoon Theory has swooned away.

THE SPIRITUAL RESURRECTION THEORY

Then there is the view of the Jehovah's Witnesses, which is the spiritual resurrection theory. This theory also seems to be gaining currency with some theological liberals today. They say that Jesus' resurrection was not physical, but it was spiritual, and that He was just a spirit. But the Bible directly refutes this:

"Now as they said these things, Jesus Himself stood in the midst of them, and said to them, 'Peace to you.' But they were terrified and frightened, and supposed they had seen a spirit" (Luke 24:36-37).

Yes, says the Jehovah's Witnesses, they were right. What they saw was a spirit. Not so fast. Luke continues:

And He said to them, "Why are you troubled? And why do doubts arise in your hearts? Behold My hands and My feet, that it is I Myself. Handle Me and see, for a spirit does not have flesh and bones as you see I have." When He had said this, He showed them His hands and His feet. But while they still did not believe for joy, and marveled, He said to them, "Have you any food here?" So they gave Him a piece of broiled fish and some honeycomb. And He took it and ate in their presence (Luke 24:38-43).

This is not to mention the fact that if Jesus were just a ghost or spirit, what about the body? Well, the body is still in the tomb. What about the disciples who ran to the tomb when they heard that Jesus has risen? They would have gotten there, the stone would be in front of the door; and Jesus would still be in the tomb. Well, the Jehovah's Witnesses have managed to take care of that, too, with the same disregard of anything the Scripture or history teaches and they simply said that God destroyed the body. He evaporated it; it just disappeared. But there is nothing in the Bible that says anything whatsoever like that.

THE WRONG PERSON THEORY

Fourth, there is the view of the Muslims. This is the "wrong person theory." I doubt very much if you ever heard of this because, other than the Muslims, I don't know of anyone that believes it. But the Koran says of Jesus, "They slew him not nor crucified, but it appeared so unto them" (Surah 4:157). Commentators on the Koran state that somehow, on Good Friday, there was a mix-up and Judas got crucified instead of Christ. But the eyewitness accounts say that Jesus was crucified.

Second, we have Mary, His mother, standing at the foot of the Cross for all of those hours looking at

Him and weeping over her dying son. He says to her, "Mother."

According to this theory, she was confused—as were Pilate, the Sanhedrin and the disciples. Everyone was confused, including Jesus, because He then came to the disciples after He rose from the dead.

I wonder who it is they think that appeared to the disciples and said, "Behold my hands and feet?" Do they believe that Judas arose from the dead? They have the same kind of problem they tried to get rid of—someone that God raised from the dead—which He didn't do with Mohammed.

Another fatal flaw to this theory is that it doesn't coincide at all with the character of Jesus. He was a man of impeccable integrity, but according to this theory, He would be a fraud, a deceiver. Furthermore, if this theory were true, the tomb would still be occupied (but we know it's empty); Judas' body would still be in the tomb, and what about the guard? What happened to them? When the early Christians declared Jesus risen from the dead, they could have easily countered what they said and just shown them the tomb with the Roman seal still affixed. This theory doesn't fit any of the known facts in this case.

THE HALLUCINATION THEORY

Fifth, there is the hallucination theory—the theory that all of the disciples simply had hallucinations when they saw Him risen from the dead. Psychologists have pointed out that hallucinations are idiosyncratic[129]—that is, they are very personal and private, and people don't have collective hallucinations.

Jesus appeared to the people in the morning; He fixed breakfast with them. They hallucinated having breakfast. He appeared at noon, He walked with them to Emmaus, He appeared with them at suppertime several times, He appeared inside, He appeared outside. He even appeared to 500 people at one time. Not only did they see Him, but they heard Him, talked to Him, handled Him, and watched Him eat. They could not have been hallucinating all these things. Not to mention the other evidence; because having thus hallucinated that Jesus was alive and had appeared to them, they ran to the tomb and hallucinated that the tomb was empty, the guard was gone, the stone was rolled away, and the grave clothes were missing.

Then they began to preach that Jesus rose from the dead. If that were the case, this hallucination would be contagious. They declared that "You, Sanhedrin, you have taken with wicked hands and you have slain the Prince of Life and Glory and God has raised Him from the dead." So, the Sanhedrin ran down to the tomb, and they had the same hallucination. They hallucinated that it was empty, too.

Then the Romans, seeing there was a tumult made, went down and checked things out and talked to the guard. The guards all had hallucinations that the tomb was empty. This is all too ridiculous, obviously. It doesn't deal with any of the evidence.

THE WRONG TOMB THEORY

There is also the theory which suggests the women went to the wrong tomb. But again, we must deal with the evidence. It is conceivable that the women got mixed up, and though they had been there on Friday evening, they went to the wrong tomb. According to Kirsopp Lake, a liberal biblical scholar who taught at Harvard (1914-37), this was conceivable in that there were so many tombs around Jerusalem. But I have been to that tomb, and there aren't any tombs around it—nor were there tombs around it at the time of Christ.

If this theory were correct, the women went to the wrong tomb, and Peter and John (by themselves), ran to the wrong tomb, and then the disciples came and they went to the wrong tomb. Joseph of Arimathaea, who owned the tomb, naturally would want to see what happened, and yet he, too, went to the wrong tomb. Of course, the Sanhedrin also was concerned, and they went to the wrong tomb. And then, of course, the angel came down, and the angel went to the wrong tomb—but what does an angel know about tombs?

Of course, all the while there were the guards saying, "Hey, fellows, we're over here." They, at least, were at the right tomb. Again, this is obviously a wrong theory, and it doesn't answer any of the facts.

If the women and everyone else went to the wrong tomb and started proclaiming Christ risen from the dead, what would the Sanhedrin do? Why, they would go to the right tomb. They would tell the soldiers to roll back the stone. They would say, "Bring Him out." Then they would hang His corpse up by the heels in the town square in Jerusalem, and they would say, "There is your glorious Prince of Life. Take a good whiff of His rotting corpse." That would have been the end of Christianity right then and there.

THE LEGEND THEORY

Lastly, there is the legend theory. This is the idea that the "myth" of Christ rising from the dead just sort of gradually grew up over the decades and centuries. This view was popular in the nineteenth century. That was back when they said that the Gospels were written in the second or even the third century by people other than the apostles. But all of that has collapsed in the last 30 or 40 years. Now even the late Bishop John A. T. Robinson of England, one of the most blatant critics, wrote a book pointing out that the conservative scholars were right all along and that the Gospels were written by the men whose names they bear, and in the times we have said they were written. Robinson said near the end of his life that he believed that all the Gospels, including John, were written before 70 A.D.[130]

Furthermore, as stated above, secular historians point out that the Church of Jesus Christ began in 30 A.D. in Jerusalem, because the apostles preached the Resurrection. Jesus and the Resurrection were the central thrust of their teaching, so there was no time for myth-making or legend-spinning. As Peter said, "For we did not follow cunningly devised fables when we made known to you the power and coming of our Lord Jesus

Christ, but were eyewitnesses of His majesty" (2 Peter 1:16). John said, speaking of Jesus, "the Word of life": "That which was from the beginning, which we have heard, which we have seen with our eyes, which we have looked upon, and our hands have handled, concerning the Word of life...we declare to you" (1 John 1:1, 3:b).

What's more, we know how all of the apostles died. They were crucified and stoned and cut up. All this was done to them...supposedly for believing a legend which hadn't even yet developed, and which wasn't going to develop for another 100 or 150 years. That's absurd. It doesn't deal with any of the factual information. It doesn't deal with what the Sanhedrin, the Jews, and Romans would have done.

In his book, *The Historical Jesus*, Gary Habermas points out that there are 18 different first or second century pagan (or at least non-Christian) writers, who present more than a hundred facts about the birth of Christ, His life, teachings, miracles, crucifixion, resurrection and ascension. These names were listed in the transcript of our television special. They include Josephus, Tacitus, Thallus, Phlegon, Pliny the Younger, Suetonius, Emperor Trajan, Emperor Hadrian, the Talmud, Lucian, Mara Bar-Serapion, and so on.[131] This is no legend that built up over the centuries. It began at the beginning.

"MIRACLES DON'T HAPPEN"

Some people begin with the assumption that miracles don't happen; therefore, Christ could not have risen from the dead. But this doesn't explain any of the facts.

It is also circular logic. It is merely a presupposition that disallows the possibility of the Resurrection. Who is open-minded here? Surely not the person who rejects the Resurrection out of hand because they know miracles don't happen. How can anyone know they don't happen? It is an illogical assumption.

BUT CHRIST HAS RISEN FROM THE DEAD

But the truth is that Christ rose from the dead. The greatest problem mankind has ever faced, generation after generation, century after century, millennia after millennia, has been solved by Jesus. Death has been with us since the fall of man, and always people have asked, "If a man dies, will he rise again?" Jesus Christ has given us irrefutable evidence that the answer is "yes."

The greatest efforts of the most brilliant, unbelieving skeptical minds of the last 2,000 years to disprove the Resurrection have all come to naught. There is not one of them that could stay afloat in a debate for fifteen minutes when the evidence is given a fair examination.

There are other evidences I could discuss at length, if space permitted. I will mention them but briefly. Most notable is the transformation of the Sabbath from the Jewish Saturday to the Christian Sunday. The Resurrection took place amidst Jews who were committed and zealous Sabbatarians. How is it that suddenly the Christian Church changed from the seventh day Sabbath to the first day? Because the resurrection of Jesus Christ from the dead happened on the first day of the week.

For these Jews who believed in Jesus, and all the early Christians were Jews, to switch over from strict observance of Saturday as their holy Sabbath to Sunday as the all-important "the Lord's day," as it is called in the New Testament, was a monumental shift. The Resurrection was the cause of that shift. Christians have been worshiping Jesus Christ on Sunday from the very beginning until the present.

Dan Brown claims that "Christianity honored the Jewish Sabbath of Saturday, but Constantine shifted it to coincide with the pagan's veneration of the sun."[132] It is true that Sunday is so-named because of the sun. It is true that Constantine made the change official, but what he is leaving out is this: Christians worshiped Jesus on Sunday (on the Lord's day) from the very beginning—to honor His resurrection. Constantine just made official what Christians had been doing all along.

CONCLUSION

The Apostle Paul had to deal with a first century false teaching going around in the Church at Corinth. Some of the members of that church were claiming that there was no resurrection of the dead, which would imply that Jesus had not risen from the dead. Paul then wrote the following words, which have assured tens of millions of Christians down through the centuries:

> And if Christ is not risen, then our preaching is empty and your faith is also empty. . . . And if Christ is not risen, your faith is futile; you are still in your sins! Then also those who have

fallen asleep in Christ have perished. If in this life only we have hope in Christ, we are of all men the most pitiable. But now Christ is risen from the dead, and has become the firstfruits of those who have fallen asleep (I Corinthians 15:14, 17-20).

The Christian faith is based on the witness of history. Attacks on Christ come and go. But the facts of Jesus Christ, the divine Savior who came from Heaven to save us, remain.

6

Who Is This Jesus?

"He said to them, 'But who do you say that I am?'"

—MATTHEW 16:15

The most important question *The Da Vinci Code* raises is this: Who really is Jesus Christ? Dan Brown would have us believe that Jesus was just a man—a very special man, but just a man. For example, here is some of the dialogue in the book between Leigh Teabing, the historian expert, with Sophia Nevue, a French cryptologist with the police force. They just referred to the Nicene Council of 325 (which produced the Nicene Creed):

        "My dear," Teabing declared, "until that

moment in history, Jesus was viewed by his followers as a mortal prophet...a great and powerful man, but a man nonetheless. A mortal."

"Not the Son of God?"

"Right," Teabing said. "Jesus' establishment as 'the Son of God' was officially proposed and voted on by the Council of Nicea."

"Hold on. You're saying Jesus' divinity was the result of a vote?"

"A relatively close vote at that," Teabing added. "Nonetheless, establishing Christ's divinity was critical to the further unification of the Roman empire and to the new Vatican power base. By officially endorsing Jesus as the Son of God, Constantine turned Jesus into a deity who existed beyond the scope of the human world, an entity whose power was unchallengeable. This not only precluded further pagan challenges to Christianity, but now the followers of Christ were able to redeem themselves only via the established sacred channel—the Roman Catholic Church."[133]

As we have already pointed out: From the very beginning, Christians worshiped Jesus as divine. The Jews handed Him over to be killed because He claimed to be divine. Furthermore, it was not a close vote. Only two voted for Arianism. All the others voted against. On top of that, Dan Brown doesn't seem to realize there are hundreds of millions of Christians who are not part of the Roman Catholic Christians—as in Protestants or Orthodox Christians.

THE CHARACTER OF CHRIST

What kind of a person was Christ? Classical philosophers and ethicists, such as Cicero, Plato, Socrates and others, often violated their own maxims and even endorsed various forms of iniquity. They were the wisest men of Greece and Rome, yet some of them sanctioned slavery, oppression, revenge, infanticide or exposure of infants, polygamy, concubines, homosexuality and other vices—but not so with Christ. Said one skeptic: But how is it with Christ? He fully carried out His perfect doctrine in His life and conduct. He both was and did that which He taught. He was His own credential. Sidney Lanier, the poet, put it this way:

What "if" or "yet", what mole, what flaw, what lapse,
What least defect or shadow of defect,
What rumor, tattled by an enemy,
Of inference loose, what lack of grace
Even in torture's grasp, or sleep's, or death's, --
Oh, what amiss may I forgive in Thee,
Jesus, good Paragon, thou Crystal Christ?[134]

No one has ever been able to find any flaw in that Crystal Christ. I remember when another anti-Jesus work of fiction came out—*The Last Temptation of Christ*—which presented an imaginary Jesus, who was quite the sinner. One of the commentators opposed to the movie said of its creator: "Here is Martin (four marriages) Scorsese dragging Jesus Christ down to Martin's level."

In Dan Brown's book, he "de-deifies" Jesus (reducing Him to a mere man), and he elevates a Jesus-worshiper (Mary Magdalene) to a form of deity—the goddess, whom the protagonist of the book worships at the end of *The Da Vinci Code*. But Brown can do this only by resorting to false history.

In the finest of diamonds we may find flaws, but none in the Son of God. All human heroes have feet of clay, sometimes up to their hips or armpits, but not so with Christ:

> • "Which of you convicts Me of sin?" (John 8:46), Christ said. No one stepped forward to take the challenge.
> • That one who condemned Him to die said, "I find no fault in this Man" (Luke 23:4).
> • And he who betrayed Him said, "I have betrayed the innocent blood" (Matthew 27:4).
> • He that crucified Him said, "Certainly this was a righteous man" (Luke 23:47).

This was the Son of God. No. No one has found fault with Christ.

LITERARY MEN'S OPINIONS

The greatest of minds and intellects have believed in Him, despite the fact that so many today would say "nay."

> • Experts who examine these things tell us that William Shakespeare probably had the greatest intellect of anyone who ever lived. They based that partly upon his writings and the vastness of his

vocabulary. Shakespeare demonstrated a larger vocabulary than any other writer in history, and the bard of Stratford on Avon said this:

"I commend my soul into the hands of God my Creator, hoping and assuredly believing, through the merits of Jesus Christ my Savior to be made partaker of Life everlasting."[135]

• Again, Lord Byron, English poet and one of the greatest literary geniuses of recent centuries, said, "If ever man was God or God man, Jesus Christ was both."[136]

• W. E. Biederwolf said this:

"A man who can read the New Testament and not see that Christ claims to be more than a man can look all over the sky at high noon on a cloudless day and not see the sun."[137]

• Noah Webster, a great Christian and a great intellect, when asked if he could comprehend Christ said:

"I should be ashamed to acknowledge Him as my Saviour if I could comprehend Him—He would be no greater than myself. Such is my sense of sin, and consciousness of my inability to save myself, that I feel I need a superhuman Saviour—one so great and glorious that I cannot comprehend Him."[138]

Yes, we may apprehend Christ, but we cannot comprehend Him and embrace Him or wrap our mind around Him, or we would be greater than He.

JESUS—THE GIFT OF GOD

At one time I was far away from God, immersed in the sin and pleasures of the world. But one Sunday morning, after having attended a party late the night before, I was awakened by a preacher on my radio alarm clock, whereas there had been music on that radio station the night before. Not interested in spiritual things, I was about to spring out of bed and change the station, but he said a few things that caught my attention. In striking contrast to what the world thinks—to what I thought—the preacher declared that the Bible says, "The wages of sin is death...but...the gift of God is eternal life in Jesus Christ our Lord" (Romans 6:23).

I will never forget the first day I heard that incredible statement. I was astonished that he had the audacity to say that God wanted to give me Heaven as a gift. I thought that the man must be mad. Being, of course, a great authority on theological matters—at the age of 24—I figured that he didn't know what he was talking about. After all, who was he but a doctor of theology, a pastor of one of our nation's great churches with a worldwide radio ministry? How could that compare to my vast theological knowledge? Why, I could even find my Bible—given enough time.

JESUS—THE ONE WHO CANCELS THE SINNER'S DEATH SENTENCE

How well I remember that day when I first discovered the truth about myself, when the Holy Spirit opened my eyes to see myself as I really was. I was arraigned before the bar of God's judgment. Justice accused me, and the scales tipped precipitously against me. The angels were empanelled as juries and brought in a sentence of death against me. The Judge looked me sternly in the face and said, "I pronounce that you shall die. Do you have anything to say for yourself before the sentence of eternal death is pronounced upon you?"

For the first time in all of my self-righteous life I was speechless. The Judge brought down his gavel, and the sentence was pronounced. Eternal death descended upon me, and I stood on the scaffold of God's judgment. I felt the black cap of eternal death placed upon my head and about to be pulled down over my eyes. My heart pounded within my breast and my knees grew weak. I abandoned all hope, as I was about to sink into everlasting perdition.

Suddenly, I heard a cry—a voice—which said, "Stay. Let not that man descend into the pit." I looked and there came at a great run One whose face was flecked with blood, whose hands were pierced, who said, "Surely he deserves to die, but the spear pierced My side instead. Surely he deserves to descend into the pit, but there in the blackness of midday at Calvary, I descended into the pit for him. All that he deserves I have properly taken. Now let him go free."

That day my life was transformed. I rose, went forth, and followed Him. My heart for these past 50 years has overflowed with gratitude and love for Christ, for I know that within my soul there is a certificate that says, "The gift of God is eternal life through Jesus Christ my Lord."

My conversion to Christ and all the conversions mentioned above are similar to the healing of the blind man that we find in John 9. Jesus encountered a man blind from birth, and He gave him the gift of sight. The healing was done on the Sabbath, so it caused a controversy among the Jews, to whom a violation of the Sabbath was an egregious offense. Some thought Him a sinner, since He healed on the Sabbath; others asked how could He do this apart from the power of God.

When they asked the formerly blind man about this, he gave them a beautiful straightforward testimony: "Whether He is a sinner or not, I do not know. One thing I do know: Though I was blind, now I see." Every true Christian can echo that last sentiment: "though I was blind, now I see."

Through the years I have seen hundreds, even thousands, come to Christ at the church where I serve as senior pastor. All of them have a story to tell of one kind or another. Some are more dramatic than others, but as long as they truly come to Jesus Christ, they are on their way to Heaven. I think of a man whose whole family rejoiced when he was converted. His daughter told my wife: "I have a new daddy, and I like him better than the old one."

Of course, the finest testimonies are from those who grow up in Christian homes and love and serve the Lord faithfully all of their lives, without ever going the path of the Prodigal Son. It doesn't matter how you come to Christ; what matters is that you come to Christ.

DISTORTIONS OF CHRISTIANITY

Unfortunately, through the ages, the devil has distorted Christianity so much that the Gospel has often been obscured. People, even lifetime churchgoers, often don't have a clue as to what real Christianity is all about. So just exactly what is Christianity? Sometimes, the "Christianity" being attacked by our culture today is such a false, twisted caricature that it bears little resemblance to the true faith. Indeed it ought to be attacked. Recently, a lesbian who claimed to be a Christian came "out of the closet," declaring war on historic Christianity—the religion of the Cross. It turns out that as a child she had been placed naked on a cross by an adult—for some twisted, religious reason. Today she resents and rejects the Cross of Christ as the means of salvation. Woe to the person who did this terrible misdeed, for it has caused her to reject a "straw man" of Christianity, not the real thing.

But God's timeless truths about the salvation He offers us in Christ are not made null by the sins of professing Christians. Even if the entire official Church were to become apostate, that would not nullify the Gospel. Therefore, I want to devote the rest of this chapter to the purpose of clarifying what true Christianity really is.

The basic message of Christianity is not "do," but "done." "It is done" were the last words of Christ before commending His soul to the Father. It is done. It is finished. It is complete. It is accomplished (to quote Mel Gibson's film, *The Passion of the Christ*). It is enough. *Tetelestai* is the Greek word Jesus said when He breathed

His last. This Greek word was often used in economic transactions, and it means "paid in full." Jesus Christ paid the penalty for our sins. The atonement is completed, and now, all who trust in Him may have eternal life freely.

JESUS: "YOU MUST BE PERFECT"

I remember twenty-five years or so ago, my wife and I were invited to a dinner at the home of one of our church families. There must have been about 10 or 15 people present. There was a long table and I was invited to sit down near one end of the table; my wife was seated near the other end. Across from me was the mother of the hostess, a lady about 65 or 70, and she said to me, "Oh, Rev. Kennedy, I am so happy to be seated across from you, because I've always wanted to ask a minister a question."

And I said, "Well, fine, I will be glad to try and answer it. Don't make it too hard or I'll have to get up and go ask my wife. But what is it?"

She said, "How good does a person have to be, to be good enough to get into Heaven?"

Now, that's a question many people ought to ask themselves. So many do not even bother to do so, but at least this woman had the intelligence to realize that if one was going to get into Heaven by being good, one should intelligently ask how good is good enough. What is the passing grade in this course? Is it 70 or 75 or 80 or 60 or 50 or what is it?

And I said, "Oh, is that your question? Well,

that's easy."

And her face just broke out in a huge smile. She said, "Do you mean you know?"

And I said, "Of course. That's the simplest possible question."

She said, "You will never know how relieved I am. I have been worrying about that for years."

I said, "Well, you will never need to worry about the answer to that question ever again, because from this day forward, you will know."

She said, "Oh, I'm so glad I came." She said, "What is it?"

I said, "Jesus said it very clearly, very understandably. He said, 'Therefore you shall be perfect, just as your Father in heaven is perfect'" (Matthew 5:48).

The smile left her face. She looked like one of those cartoon characters that had been hit by a skillet. Her face just sort of fell onto the table, and she sat there silently for a long time. Then she said, "I think I'm going to worry about that more than ever."

I replied, "Dear lady, I did not go into the ministry to make people worry, but far from it—to deliver them from their worries." I was then happy to share with her the Gospel of Jesus Christ, that while none of us is perfect, and none of us has lived up to God's standard, and all of us have fallen short, Jesus Christ came to do what we have been unable to do.

The Law of God shows us the helplessness and hopelessness of our condition. The Law declares to us that if you offend in one point, you are guilty already. In fact, the Law would even take us to the end of the trial, that we might see the outcome of our judgment. Would you like for me to tell you how your encounter with the judgment of God will come out? Christ has already told you. He says, "You are condemned already."

There it is—a preview of coming attractions. You already know the end. If you are trying to gain admission into Paradise by keeping the Law and doing good works and being the best person you can be—then let me tell you that the verdict is already in. You have failed. You have flunked. Your grade is "F," and the declaration of the Judge is, "Depart from me, you cursed, into everlasting fire prepared for the devil and his angels" (Matthew 25:41).

Again, Christianity is good news. Jesus died for us, in our place, and offers us the free gift of eternal life. Thus, God has made salvation available to us by His grace, which is unmerited favor.

JESUS GIVES US TWO OPTIONS

There are two groups of people. Those who are trying to work their way into Heaven and those who have trusted in Christ alone for the salvation of their eternal souls. In which group are you? You cannot escape, my friends. There are some decisions that are impossible not to make. This is one of those. You will decide this day. You cannot avoid it.

There are some decisions in life with two options. While we are deciding which of those options we will choose, we discover that we are already in one of them.

For example, your car stalls on a railroad track and a train is coming towards you. Two options now loom before you. You can leap from your car and save your life, or you can stay in your car and try to save both life and auto. As you weigh the dangers and gains involved in those two options, the inevitable fact is that you have already chosen one: you are in your car and the train is still coming.

Likewise, today you have two options: life or death, but while you consider the choice, you have already chosen one, for you are already in that state of death into which every soul is born. Meanwhile, the judgment train of God comes on apace. You must choose.

The Gospel is the greatest offer ever made. I tell you that the day will come when the offer will be recalled and the time of grace will end forever, but now the sun of His grace is shining and the offer of His love and mercy and the free gift waits for you. There are some who have feebly accepted that offer, but they lack the assurance that they are going to Heaven, but He promises in His Word, through His servant John: "These things I have written to you who believe in the name of the Son of God, that you may *know* that you have eternal life" (1 John 5:13) [emphasis mine].

Dear one, have you ever truly yielded your life to Christ? Have you ever truly surrendered yourself to Him? "There is life for a look at the crucified One." Won't you come to Him and yield your heart? Say, "Lord Jesus Christ, melt this cold, hard heart of mine. I want you as my Savior and I want to be your child. Lord Jesus Christ, I yield myself to You. I open my heart. Come in and cleanse and melt and woo my heart to You. Bind me with bonds of love to Your side. Help me, henceforth, from this day forward, to love You supremely, to serve You faithfully until I come to see You face-to-face. In Your name I pray. Amen."

If you prayed that prayer in sincerity, you have begun the greatest adventure on which you could ever embark. I would strongly urge you to begin to read the Bible every day and to pray. If you have never read the Bible before, start with the Gospel of John (the fourth book of the New Testament).

I also urge you to get involved with a Bible-based, Bible-believing church. If you would like a free book to help you become established in the Christian faith, write to me and ask for *Beginning Again*.[139]

Once we know Jesus as our personal Lord and Savior, our "thank you" to Him for His gift of salvation is to serve Him in every area of our life. Good works will naturally flow from our lives, as good apples grow naturally on a good apple tree.

CONCLUSION

Suppose there were a novel where the entire premise was built on an assassination attempt against the King of the United States of America. Why, that's absurd, you say! Perhaps people might enjoy the story as pure fiction, but nobody would lend historical credence to its "facts," because everyone knows we have no king. Yet *The Da Vinci Code* is every bit as fictitious as this hypothetical plotline, if you are familiar with a few basics of early Christian history. The only reason Dan Brown can get away with intimating a factual basis for his story is because there is such widespread ignorance of Christian history, including these facts:

• The Gospels in the Bible are based on eyewitness testimony and have far more historical credibility than spurious documents written in the second, third, or fourth centuries by, if you will, Christian cults.

• The Christian emperor Constantine did not create the Bible, nor did he declare its canon, nor was he the first to declare Jesus divine.

• Jesus was worshiped as divine from the very beginning. Those who believed in Him sealed their testimony with their own blood. They could not deny what they saw with their own eyes and touched with their own hands.

• Jesus was never married to anyone because He will marry His bride (the Church) at the end of time (Revelation 19:6-10).

The Da Vinci Code should be taken as a 100 percent novel. By-and-large if you treat its "facts" as fiction, you are closer to the truth than if you treat its "facts" as facts.

When the movie trailers for *The Da Vinci Code* were running, they declared, "Seek the truth." That is one statement that we would totally agree with. Seek the truth. Seek with an open mind. See why tens of millions have discovered that Jesus Christ is who He says He was—God in human flesh—who came down from Heaven to redeem human beings.

When you seek, you will find. When you seek the

truth, you will find Jesus Christ, for He Himself declared, "I am...the truth" (John 14:6).

Even to this day, people use the phrase "gospel" as synonymous with "truth." The gospel—as found in the four Gospels—is indeed "the gospel truth." It has stood the test of time and weathered all sorts of attacks—the latest of which is what we call "the Da Vinci Myth." In time, the Da Vinci Myth will be discarded in the dustbin of history, while the Gospel Truth will continue to spread abroad. The tragedy is that in the interim, some people will miss Heaven because they reject the gospel truth and believe the Da Vinci myth.

Soli Deo Gloria.

ENDNOTES

1 Dan Brown, *The Da Vinci Code* (New York, et al.: Doubleday, 2003), 1.

2 Roelof van den Broek and Wouter J. Hanegraaff, ed.s, *Gnosis and Hermeticism from Antiquity to Modern Times* (Albany: State University of New York Press, 1998), 9.

3 Ibid., 4.

4 James M. Robinson, gen. ed., *The Nag Hammadi Library in English* (San Francisco: HarperSanFrancisco, A Division of HarperCollinsPublishers, 1978/1990), 5.

5 Epiphanius, quoted in ibid., 5.

6 Irenaeus, "Traditions of the Elders," *Against Heresies*, IV.32.1, quoted in Eberhard Arnold, ed., *The Early Christians in Their Own Words* (Farmington, Penn.: Plough Publishing House, 1997), 142.

7 James M. Robinson, gen. ed., *The Nag Hammadi Library in English* (San Francisco: HarperSanFrancisco, A Division of HarperCollinsPublishers, 1978 / 1990), 158.

8 Transcript of an interview with Erwin Lutzer (Ft. Lauderdale: Coral Ridge Ministries-TV, 2004).

9 Dan Brown, *The Da Vinci Code* (New York, et al.: Doubleday, 2003), 231.

10 Ibid.

11 Ibid.

12 Ibid.

13 If someone argues that there are some discrepancies among the Greek manuscripts, my reply is that at worst that impacts 3-4% of the content of the manuscripts we have today, and none of the minor variations within the texts (minor word changes or word rearrangements which don't affect the Greek meaning or spelling discrepancies) impact any major doctrines in the least—-or if they do, those doctrines are clearly upheld in other verses over which there is no question at all.

14 Dan Brown, *The Da Vinci Code* (New York, et al.: Doubleday, 2003), 233.

15 Jim Garlow and Peter Jones, *Cracking Da Vinci's Code* (Colorado Springs: Victor, an imprint of Cook Communications, 2004), 96.

16 Gary Habermas, *The Historical Jesus: Ancient Evidence for the Life of Christ* (Joplin, Mo: College Press Publishing Company, 1996), 245.

17 Paul L. Maier, quoted in D. James Kennedy, *Who Is This Jesus* (Ft. Lauderdale: Coral Ridge Ministries-TV, 2000), a video.

18 Amy-Jill Levine, quoted in ibid.

19 Amy-Jill Levine, quoted in D. James Kennedy, *Who Is This Jesus: Is He Risen?* (Ft. Lauderdale: Coral Ridge Ministries-TV, 2001), a video.

20 Sam Lamerson, quoted in ibid.

21 Dan Brown, *The Da Vinci Code* (New York, et al.: Doubleday, 2003), 345.

22 Ibid., 232.

23 The Bible declares that no murderer has eternal life (1 John 3:15). That means that no one who claims to be saved and goes out and commits murder is truly saved. (That includes Albino monks, of whom there are none in Opus Dei). We know in history that some who have claimed to be Christians have murdered in the name of Christ, to wit, the Spanish Inquisition. But that doesn't mean what they did was right. It certainly wasn't correct from a biblical perspective. (In fact, some of those killed in the Inquisition were Bible-believing Christians.) Furthermore, that doesn't mean that such murderers went to Heaven. A former murderer who repents and puts his faith in the salvation of the Lord can be saved, e.g., King David (Psalm 51). But no one who is truly saved will then go out and commit murder.

24 Hank Hanegraaff & Paul L. Maier, *The Da Vinci Code: Fact or Fiction?* (Wheaton, Ill.: Tyndale House Publishers, Inc., 2004), 12.

25 Ibid.

26 Dan Brown, *The Da Vinci Code* (New York, et al.: Doubleday, 2003), 1.

27 Ibid., 345.

28 Ibid., 233.

29 Will Durant, *Caesar and Christ: A History of Roman Civilization and of Christianity From Their Beginnings to a.d. 325* (New York: Simon and Schuster, 1944; renewed 1972), 652.

30 The Nicene Creed in Felician A. Foy, ed., *The 1988 Catholic Almanac* (Huntington, Ind.: Our Sunday Visitor Publishing Division, 1987), 199-200.

31 Paraphrase of Phillip Cary, "The Logic of Trinitarian Doctrine," *Religious and Theological Studies Fellowship Bulletin* (September/October 1995): 2, cited in Roger E. Olson's and Christopher A. Hall, The Trinity (Grand Rapids: Wm. B. Eerdmans Publishing Co., 2002), 46.

32 Jim Garlow and Peter Jones, *Cracking Da Vinci's Code* (Colorado Springs: Victor, an imprint of Cook Communications, 2004), 94.

33 Paul Maier, quoted in D. James Kennedy, *Who Is This Jesus* (Ft. Lauderdale: Coral Ridge Ministries-TV, 2000), a video.

34 D. A. Carson, quoted in ibid.

35 Bruce Metzger, quoted in ibid.

36 N. T. Wright, quoted in ibid.

37 Sam Lamerson, quoted in ibid.

38 N. T. Wright, quoted in ibid.

39 Darrell L. Bock, *Breaking the Da Vinci Code* (Nashville: Thomas Nelson, 2004), 131.

40 Dan Brown, *The Da Vinci Code* (New York, et al.: Doubleday, 2003), 231.

41 James M. Robinson, gen. ed., *The Nag Hammadi Library in English* (San Francisco: HarperSanFrancisco, A Division of HarperCollinsPublishers, 1978 / 1990), 148.

42 Erwin Lutzer, *The Da Vinci Deception* (Wheaton, Ill.: Tyndale, 2004), 67.

43 Sam Lamerson, quoted in D. James Kennedy, *Who Is This Jesus* (Ft. Lauderdale: Coral Ridge Ministries-TV, 2000), a video.

44 Transcript of Richard Abanes interview (Ft. Lauderdale: Coral Ridge Ministries-TV, 2005).

45 James M. Robinson, gen. ed., *The Nag Hammadi Library in English* (San Francisco: HarperSanFrancisco, A Division of HarperCollinsPublishers, 1978/1990), 148.

46 Ben Witherington III, *The Gospel Code* (Downers Grove, Ill.: IVP, 2004), 37.

47 Transcript of an interview with Gary Habermas (Ft. Lauderdale: Coral Ridge Ministries-TV, 2004).

48 Hank Hanegraaff & Paul L. Maier, *The Da Vinci Code: Fact or Fiction?* (Wheaton, Ill.: Tyndale House Publishers, Inc., 2004), 34.

49 Dan Brown, *The Da Vinci Code* (New York, et al.: Doubleday, 2003), 232.

50 Carl E. Olson and Sandra Miesel, *The Da Vinci Hoax: Exposing the Errors in The Da Vinci Code* (San Francisco: Ignatius Press, 2004), 145-146.

51 Dan Brown, *The Da Vinci Code* (New York, et al.: Doubleday, 2003), 1.

52 Hank Hanegraaff & Paul L. Maier, *The Da Vinci Code: Fact or Fiction?* (Wheaton, Ill.: Tyndale House Publishers, Inc., 2004), 35.

53 There is a sense in which the "end days" have been with us from the era of the New Testament to the present. Peter says in Acts 2:17 that these predicted for the "last days" were being fulfilled in those days. So we are not saying that the very end is necessarily right around the corner. Also, the author of Hebrews says, "in these last days"—referring to his own day (Hebrews 1:2). So are these the last days? Yes, and they have been since the New Testament to the present.

54 C.S. Lewis, *Mere Christianity* (New York: MacMillan Publishing Company, 1960), 51.

55 Dan Brown, *The Da Vinci Code* (New York, et al.: Doubleday, 2003), 248.

56 Ibid., 235.

57 R. C. Sproul in D. James Kennedy, *The Bible: Fable, Fraud or Fact?* (Ft. Lauderdale: Coral Ridge Ministries, 1994), a video.

58 Don Feder, "Annihilation of the soul at the Harvard Divinity School" Los Angelos: Creators Syndicate, April 4, 1994.

59 Ibid.

60 Ibid.

61 Thomas J. Billitteri, "The Gospels: Was Jesus Misquoted?" *St. Petersburg Times*, January 29, 1994, 1A.

62 Robert Funk, Roy Hoover, and the Jesus Seminar, *The Five Gospels; What Did Jesus Really Say?* (New York: Macmillan, 1993).

63 "Jesus: A Divorced Father of Three? Latest Blast of Post Christianity Selling Like Mad in Australia, U.S." *The Christian Challenge*, November, 1992. Reprinted in *The Christian News*, Nov. 16, 1992.

64 Richard N. Ostling, "Jesus Christ, Plain and Simple" *Time*, January 10, 1994, 38.

65 N.T. Wright, "The New, Unimproved Jesus: An eminent scholar investigates the recent, intriguing attempts to find the 'real' Jesus," *Christianity Today*, September 13, 1993, 22-26.

66 Francis Martin in D. James Kennedy, *Who Is This Jesus* (Ft. Lauderdale: Coral Ridge Ministries, 2000), a video.

67 James Montgomery Boice in D. James Kennedy, *The Bible: Fable, Fraud or Fact?* (Ft. Lauderdale: Coral Ridge Ministries, 1994), a video.

68 Ibid.

69 R. C. Sproul in ibid.

70 Michael J. Wilkins and J.P. Moreland, ed.s, *Jesus Under Fire: Modern Scholarship Reinvents the Historical Jesus* (Grand Rapids: Zondervan, 1995).

71 *The U.S. Book of Facts Statistics & Information for 1968* (New York: An Essandess Special Edition, 1967). Officially published by the U.S. Government as Statistical Abstract of the United States Issued by the Bureau of the Census, U.S. Department of Commerce, 42.

72 *The World Almanac and Book of Facts 1995* (New York: Funk & Wagnalls Corporation, 1994), 729.

73 *The U.S. Book of Facts Statistics & Information for 1968* (New York: An Essandess Special Edition, 1967). Officially published by the U.S. Government as Statistical Abstract of the United States Issued by the Bureau of the Census, U.S. Department of Commerce, 5.

74 *The World Almanac and Book of Facts 1995* (New York: Funk & Wagnalls Corporation, 1994), 373.

75 *World Almanac 2006* (New York: World Almanac Books, 2006), 714.

76 *World Almanac and Book of Facts 1980* (New York: Newspaper Enterprise Association, Inc., 1979), 351.

77 *World Almanac 2006* (New York: World Almanac Books, 2006), 714.

78 "Statistical Record of Membership," PCUSA, *The Presbyterian Lay Committee*, Springfield, Penn., fax dated September 1, 1995.

79 Membership size from Presbyterian Church (U.S.A.) website at http://www.pcusa.org/navigation/whoweare.htm

80 Alister McGrath, "Why Evangelicalism Is the Future of Protestantism," *Christianity Today*, June 19, 1995, 18.

81 Lutheran Professor Leif Vaage of Lima, Peru. Cited by Gayle White, "Christ Was 'No Goody Two Shoes' Says Organizer of Jesus Seminar," *The Atlanta Journal*, September 30, 1989.

82 Robert Funk quoted in ibid.

83 Ibid.

84 Transcript of an interview with Adam McManus (KSLR, San Antonio) (Ft. Lauderdale: Coral Ridge Ministries-TV, 2006).

85 Dan Brown, *The Da Vinci Code* (New York et al: Doubleday, 2003), 309.

86 Biblical archaeologist Joseph Free says that in the temples of the ancient Canaanites—the people whom God told the Israelites to drive out or destroy because of their depravity—practiced "debased sex worship," which resulted in child sacrifice. Their temples were "places of vice." (Joseph Free, *Archaeology and*

Bible History (Wheaton: Scripture Press, 1969), 122). The eminent archaeologist, W. F. Albright, concurs:

"In no country has so relatively great a number of figurines of the naked goddess of fertility, some distinctly obscene, been found. Nowhere does the cult of serpents appear so strongly. The two goddesses Astarte (Ashtaroth) and Anath are called the great goddesses which conceive but do not bear! Sacred courtesans and eunuch priests were excessively common. Human sacrifice was well-known . . . the erotic aspects of their cult must have sunk to extremely sordid depth of social degradation." [Quoted in Merrill Unger, Archaeology and the Old Testament (Grand Rapids: Zondervan, 1979), 75.] God commanded the Hebrews to clean all this up, and not to practice it.

87 Aruna Gnanadason, quoted in Susan Cyre, "Women's conference re-imagines new god," *Rutherford*, August, 1994,19.

88 Ibid.

89 "Onward Christian Sophists," *National Review*, April 18, 1994, 19.

90 George Archibald, "Anti-Vatican groups says Bible backs it," *Washington Times*, September 1, 1995, A1.

91 C. S. Lewis, *The Screwtape Letters with Screwtape Proposes a Toast*, Revised Edition (New York: Collier Books, Macmillan Publishing Company, 1961, 1982), 12.

92 C. S. Lewis, *Miracles* (New York: Macmillan, 1960), 164.

93 John R. W. Stott, *The Authority of the Bible* (Downers Grove, Ill: IVP, 1974), 7, 17.

94 Ibid., 29.

95 Ibid.

96 Tertullian, quoted in ibid., 27.

97 Transcript of an interview with Erwin Lutzer (Ft. Lauderdale: Coral Ridge Ministries-TV, 2004).

98 Ibid.

99 Benjamin Breckinridge Warfield, *The Inspiration and Authority of the Bible* (Philadelphia: Presbyterian and Reformed, 1948), quoted in Norman L. Geisler and William E. Nix, A General Introduction to the Bible (Chicago: Moody Press, 1968, 1988), 38-39.

100 Edward J. Young, quoted in Paul Enns, *Moody Handbook on Theology* (Chicago: Moody Press, 1989), 160.

101 Norman L. Geisler and William E. Nix, *A General Introduction to the Bible* (Chicago: Moody Press, 1968, 1988), 39.

102 Lee Strobel in D. James Kennedy, *The Bible: Fable, Fraud or Fact?* (Ft. Lauderdale: Coral Ridge Ministries, 1994), a video.

103 Lee Strobel and Gary Poole, *Exploring The Da Vinci Code* (Grand Rapids: Zondervan, 2006).

104 Lee Strobel, *Inside the Mind of Unchurched Harry and Mary: How To Reach Friends And Family Who Avoid God And The Church* (Grand Rapids: Zondervan, 1993), 36.

105 Peter Stoner, Science Speaks (Chicago: Moody Press, 1963), p. 109. Quoted in Josh McDowell, *Evidence That Demands a Verdict* (San Bernardino, Calif.: Campus Crusade for Christ, 1972), 167.

106 Lee Strobel, *Inside The Mind Of Unchurched Harry & Mary: How To Reach Friends And Family Who Avoid God And The Church* (Grand Rapids: Zondervan Publishing House, 1993), 37.

107 Ibid.

108 Ibid.

109 Transcript of an interview with Ralph Muncaster (Ft. Lauderdale: Coral Ridge Ministries-TV, 2004).

110 Jim Garlow and Peter Jones, *Cracking Da Vinci's Code* (Colorado Springs: Victor, an imprint of Cook Communications, 2004), 133.

111 Ibid., 134.

112 Ibid., 143.

113 F. F. Bruce, *The New Testament Documents: Are They Reliable?* (Downers Grove, Ill.: IVP, 1943, 1974), 27.

114 Dan Brown, *The Da Vinci Code* (New York, et al.: Doubleday, 2003), 231.

115 Ravi Zacharias in D. James Kennedy, *The Bible: Fable, Fraud or Fact?* (Ft. Lauderdale: Coral Ridge Ministries, 1994), a video.

116 Sir Frederic G. Kenyon, *The Bible and Archaeology*, 288 f., quoted in Norman L. Geisler and William E. Nix, *A General Introduction to the Bible* (Chicago: Moody Press, 1968, 1988), 405.

117 Ravi Zacharias in D. James Kennedy, *The Bible: Fable, Fraud or Fact?* (Ft. Lauderdale: Coral Ridge Ministries, 1994), a video.

118 See Paul L. Maier, *In the Fulness of Time: A Historian Looks at Christmas, Easter, and the Early Church* (Grand Rapids: Kregel Publications, 1991), 197-205.

119 Josh McDowell, *Evidence that Demands a Verdict* (San Bernadino, Calif.: Campus Crusade for Christ, 1972, 209.

120 Quoted in ibid., 214.

121 Ibid., 223.

122 Ibid.

123 Dan Brown, *The Da Vinci Code* (New York et al: Doubleday, 2003), 231.

124 Transcript from a TV interview with Jerry Newcombe, Ft. Lauderdale, Fla., Spring 1988.

125 Josh McDowell, *Evidence That Demands a Verdict*, 179.

126 Hill's Lectures in Divinity, Vol. I, pp. 47, 48. Quoted in William Taylor, *The Miracles of Our Saviour* (New York: Hodder and Stoughton, 1890), 2122.

127 Ibid., 233.

128 Quoted in Josh McDowell, *Evidence That Demands a Verdict*, 244.

129 Ibid., 248255.

130 One of the reasons he came to believe this was because it says in John 5:2, "Now there *is* in Jerusalem by the Sheep Gate a pool..." [emphasis mine] When the Roman Titus came in 70 A.D., he thoroughly destroyed Jerusalem and much of Israel. So Robinson believed, therefore, that John, the final gospel to be was written before 70 A.D

131 Gary Habermas, *The Historical Jesus: Ancient Evidence for the Life of Christ* (Joplin, Missouri, College Press Publishing Company, 1996), 187-228.

132 Dan Brown, *The Da Vinci Code* (New York, et al.: Doubleday, 2003), 232-233.

133 Ibid., 233.

134 J. Gilchrist, *Greatest Thoughts About Jesus Christ* (New York: Richard R. Smith, Inc., 1930), 127.

135 Ibid., 117.

136 Ibid., 118.

137 Ibid., 21.

138 Ibid., 123.

139 If you would like more information to help you get grounded in the Christian faith, write to me at Coral Ridge Ministries, Box 40, Ft. Lauderdale, FL 33308 and ask for *Beginning Again*. Co-author Jerry Newcombe highly recommends a book that has helped him. It is a three-year "through-the-Bible" study guide, *Search the Scriptures*, edited by Alan Stibbs (Downers Grove, Ill.: IVP, 1949, 1974). It is now available in paperback.

INDEX